The Positive Worker

A GUIDE TO DEVELOPING A WINNING ATTITUDE AT WORK

By Blake LeVine, MSW

Published by Blake LeVine Coaching, Inc.
9517 Aegean Drive
Boca Raton, Fl 33496
Tel: (213) 304-9555
Email: blakelevinecoach@gmail.com
Website: http://www.blakelevinecoaching.com

ACKNOWLEDGEMENTS

I have had the honor of helping hundreds of business owners and workers through many stressful situations. The knowledge of learning to develop a positive attitude has allowed many to make positive progress. It is clear that corporations that have motivated, inspired, enthusiastic and cooperative teams achieve their goals.

My greatest appreciation is to the many high level executives, their staff and businesses that have allowed me to share my lessons. It has been an honor to watch companies make change together and in a way that supports continued growth.

I want to thank my wonderful wife, Jennifer, and my two children for allowing me to have a beautiful family. It is their warmth and kindness that has allowed me to help others. The greatest teams and businesses are the ones willing to learn and adapt. They come together to teach, support and help each other reach their highest potential.

CONTENTS

INTRODUCTION

You are extremely valuable. In this moment, you are working for a team. This book is here to help you learn to develop a positive attitude.

There was an article recently written about members of The Navy Seals. It detailed how their number one training lesson is to develop a huge level of optimism. They are taught that they must work to stay positive and believe in the success of their missions.

You may ask why skilled warriors with great strength spend so much time on being positive. The answer is they are placed in some of the toughest situations anyone might encounter. When they fully believe and anticipate accomplishing their goal, they are more likely to complete their assignment.

This book is a guide to help teams come together and grow their skills. The facts are; when someone in a work setting is negative, nasty, or angry it harms the whole environment. This book has been created to help each team member learn to improve their own abilities as well as work toward a higher level of success.

I have had the honor of teaching many corporations and organizations, both large and small. Over many years, I have done one-on-one coaching for many types of workers. I've helped with banking clients during the Lehman Brothers crises in 2008. I've seen companies go through structural changes and adapt to different types of leadership. It is fascinating when a team comes together and thrives in their business.

The one lesson that has maintained the same is how to find hope and optimism. I have witnessed how the attitude and effort one worker places in their job has the ability to impact hundreds of others. I have seen how team building has led to higher levels of sales, success and members enjoying their jobs.

You have the potential to make your work environment better. When you read this book, the lessons and exercises will help you develop new skills and change your thought pattern. You may find that this book becomes a tool to improve your career. It will also help your team come together in a healthier way. The group that learns to work together becomes the one that wins sales, new customers, greater productivity and achieves a balanced work environment.

CHAPTER ONE

The Value of a Positive Attitude

There were two shoe stores in a small town of 8,000 residents. Each shop had the most popular brands of sneakers, sandals, high heels and footwear. The layout of each store was similar and there was nothing unique about the design of either location.

One of the stores was run by a kind woman named Jane. She was always warm, friendly, supportive and helpful to her team. She trained her sales staff to always smile at new customers, ask how they are doing, remember them if they have been in the store before and to listen.

When one of Jane's employees hit a sales goal everyone on the floor celebrated. They would come together each week to talk about the successful accomplishments. Jane would ask the staff member who had the highest sales to speak about why it was going well. Jane also encouraged her team to offer her feedback and ways to make customers even more happy.

One staff suggested a loyalty program to encourage shoppers to return. This led to sending each customer who bought a pair of shoes a thank you card handwritten by the sales person who sold them the item. They included a gift card for $10 off their next purchase. The card also shared how much the staff member is thankful for the customers shopping at the store.

The shop continues to grow and thrive. There are many customers who speak of the warmth and kindness they find at Jane's Shoes. Many have become loyal shoppers and always go back to see their favorite sales person. Jane's has been growing and is looking to expand into an even larger location.

I did mention earlier that there were two shoe stores. What happened to the other one? It is no longer in business due to some basic mistakes. The other shoe shop was owned by a man named Tom. He opened the store and figured he would find success. Tom told his employees to sell shoes and focus on how much they sold. He was sometimes angry and took out his failures on his workers.

This led to many of the staff quitting the job. He also created a negative environment. His sales team were not properly trained and didn't enjoy working there. The few shoppers who came in didn't feel happy or warm in the store. They quickly left and most never came back.

When money became tight, most of the town chose to buy shoes at Jane's store. They didn't like Tom and felt his store was not a positive place to shop. The different attitudes would eventually spread throughout the town. It was not long before almost all of the shoppers went to Jane's and left Tom's with no business.

Tom didn't want to change and his business closed down. This allowed Jane's to have almost all of the sales in this town. It is easy to understand why one is thriving and the other failed. We can learn a great lesson from this simple story.

The value of a positive attitude is key for winning in business. When others interact with you, they feel happier around someone who is friendly, warm and kind. This is not only for sales members who work directly with customers. The best teams spread optimism throughout the whole organization.

You may begin to create a more positive attitude. One step is to look at how you respond to a situation. A supervisor tells you to complete a task. One option is to say to yourself, "I am going to do the task. I will try to do my best and complete it to the best of my ability. I am thankful to have this job and want to help my supervisor. I know that putting in my full effort helps my team and leads us to success. I will work at my highest level because it helps me grow. Even a small task is important and serves a purpose."

How many times does someone say the opposite inside? They are frustrated that they have more work to do. They become angry at the supervisor for telling them to do an additional task. They want to do the minimum to make it through the day. Many choose to be negative when at work.

When you have optimism, it helps you grow and improve your business. If you do only the minimum, who are you helping? When you don't strive for excellence, are you reaching your

potential? What happens if you develop a positive attitude and become an asset for your team?

I met a remarkable woman in 2007. I was doing coaching and therapy for business

clients and families in New York. I started to work with a woman named Lori who was

employed at Lehman Brothers. The woman began her career wanting to be a school teacher. She

had applied for a part time job at the bank and did her best. Lori worked hard and always was

helpful.

Over the next few years, she kept moving up within Lehman Brothers. When I began to work

with her, she was earning a very large salary. It was so high that it supported her husband and

two children. She spoke of having many friends and loving working at the big company.

She came in for a session when the world had shifted. It was 2008 and Lehman Brothers was

at the center of a crises. Lori told me how everyone was scared and worried about what would

happen. We spoke of how to handle it. Lori said she would keep a good attitude and be helpful to

her team. What happened next was out of her control.

The many friends and co-workers were extremely angry and upset. Many had invested their

retirement in stock of Lehman Brothers. There was fighting and chaos at the company's final

days. Lori would be a symbol of hope with how she handled the bankruptcy. She told me that

even if she lost her job she would continue to try and be warm and helpful.

What did she have to gain from being nice? The business was bankrupt and basically

everyone was going to lose their job. She didn't have anything to gain except her own sense of

self and knowing that being kind is the right way to handle her problems. What happened next

taught how important it is to keep a positive attitude.

The closure of Lehman Brothers did happen. Lori found a miracle despite the darkness. A tiny

percent of the Lehman Brothers staff was given new jobs at Barclays, which worked to take over

some of the assets of the business. It would mean only a few would survive and make it to the other bank.

Who did they choose to keep their job? Would they keep someone who was angry, complaining and focusing on the problem? They kept Lori because businesses want staff that keeps positive in the midst of a storm. They want someone like Lori who will not use a problem as an excuse to grow hostile and angry.

Lori told me that being optimistic and warm was not to keep her job. She felt bad that many of her friends lost their positions. Lori was hoping to be helpful because it is the right thing to do. She believes that you help others and are kind no matter what. Lori was able to keep working and ended up supporting her family and children.

What do we gain from learning about Lori? When something goes wrong, should you respond with anger and frustration? What does it take to be positive and develop a better attitude? We are able to learn almost anything. When a baby is born, they are capable of learning as many languages as they are taught. Once we grow older, we lose the ability to easily learn new ways of thinking. Were you taught to be positive or focus on the negative? Many grew up in households where it was normal to be negative. It does not mean you cannot shift your thinking.

Each day, we have the ability to develop new patterns. You may have heard of affirmations. These are things we tell ourselves each day. I used to have many fears and negative thoughts. I started to say to myself the following, "I feel wonderful. I feel terrific. I feel healthy." The first few weeks, I would negate what I said. Within a few months, I started to believe what I said to myself each day. I would say this in the morning and in the evening.

If I asked you right now to honestly say how you feel about your job, what would you say? Would you authentically say you are happy and enjoy the job? If you answered in a negative way, what would it mean to say something positive about your work to yourself every day?

You could say to yourself, "I feel happy to have a job. I know many are looking for a job and I feel happy that I have one. I am happy that my job gave me this book. They are trying to help me and I appreciate it. I am happy to learn how to get along with different coworkers. This is helping me grow and learn to develop my skills. I am happy that I have persisted and have been able to stay in the job."

There are easy ways to develop a more positive attitude. What you say to yourself is your reality? If you think unhappy thoughts about work, you are going to become upset. You have a choice that impacts everyone within the business. When you focus on the positive, you are leading yourself to a higher level of success.

I have seen many workers grow to be very successful. The main reason is that they are positive and try their hardest. When companies promote an employee, it is because of their optimism. We all want to be with someone who is kind, warm, helpful and supports us. You can achieve this by choosing to work on your thinking.

I finish this chapter with a simple exercise that teaches about positivity. You can fill this out either as a group or alone. You are going to answer each question with a positive response. When you are feeling upset, you can look back to this paper to remember some valuable lessons.

I am thankful I have a job because:

The best part of my job is:

One of the best lessons I have learned from my job is:

I want to grow my skills and this job will allow me to work on:

I enjoy working on a team at my job because:

One of the most fun parts of my job is:

I chose three positive things to focus on today about my job and they are:

CHAPTER TWO

Simple Steps to Improve the Environment

You have the ability to improve your work environment. This begins with taking pride in yourself. If you have a workspace, keep it clean. What would you think if you walked into a room and viewed a messy desk, papers thrown everywhere, and old food on the table?

Why should you care how your place of employment looks? The easiest answer is that everyone involved in your company matters and even small changes make a difference. This story below illustrates an example of why you must care about cleanliness.

There was an office where a team worked to print greeting cards. In the main office, five workers each had their own desk and complete their tasks in the space. Barry had been at the company for 8 years. His desk looked horrendous. There were hundreds of mock greeting cards, past project paperwork, grime on his computer and half-used soda bottles. Amy had worked there for four years and her desk is half as messy as Barry's. She also has tons of papers, greeting card mocks, as well as her old computer that broke. The third worker, Kevin, learned from Barry and Amy that is okay to have a messy desk. Kevin had tons of extra markers, papers and things spread out on his desk.

A new worker named Emily interviewed for a position. She loved greeting cards and had always wanted to work in a company that created them. Emily was excited to be able to use her creativity and be paid to do something she cares about. When she started the job she found out that her desk is with the other staff.

Emily began to wonder what to do. She did not want to keep her desk messy and filled with junk. Her family taught her to take pride in what her place looked like. Emily was worried about telling her new workers to clean their mess. It made her uncomfortable and she decided to do something different. Her choice was to keep her desk very neat. She created folders and places to put any extra papers. Each afternoon she cleaned her desk and made sure it looked tidy.

A few months later, a different manager was hired. When the new boss came in, he was shocked to see what a mess the desks were. He asked Emily why her desk was neat and everyone else's looked horrible. Emily said, "I choose to keep my desk neat because I feel more comfortable in a clean space." The other three co-workers started to laugh. One said, "Look at Emily. We should call her Mrs. Clean."

The new boss had a long talk with the staff. He said that under his supervision everyone must keep their desks clean at all times. Each of the staff was upset except Emily. She didn't have to change because she was already doing a great job. It wasn't long before Emily was given a promotion and moved up within the business.

When you take the steps to do your best always there are many rewards. This includes having pride in your work. You don't always have to be told to do the right thing. You benefit from doing your best at all times. There are several simple ways to make small changes to improve your job.

One step is to keep your environment clean. The next is to be considerate. Many businesses have a bathroom that is shared. It is helpful to keep it clean after you have used it. Please know if you leave the toilet or sink a mess the next person that uses it will be left with a negative experience. When you keep it neat, it helps your team.

You may also learn to ask questions. Many times, staff worry that they should know an answer. Their fear is being made to look stupid. This is usually not the truth. It is often better to ask questions than to to make a mistake.

I worked with a company who printed annual reports for public corporations. When they printed a report it had to be perfect. Even one mistake led to a huge amount of cost and reprinting fees. I worked with one of their staff who was seeing mistakes in the file to be printed. He was new and worried that asking his supervisor about it would make him look bad. In the beginning, he would not say anything because he was scared to mention it.

When he finally brought it up to his boss, he was told to always help the team find any mistake. If one error was found it could cost the company $5,000. His boss was apologetic for not teaching this during training. The lesson is to ask if you are not sure about something. It is better to have the right information than to guess or assume you know what to do.

There is also a great importance in learning what your role is. Many times workers do not know what they should be doing. You may ask your supervisor what are the daily goals. You may also ask the rules for taking a break, checking your email, using the phone or any other areas that you are not sure of. It is better to understand the rules than to make up your own.

I have found that the happiest workers are the ones that feel supported. You may want to develop your connection to your supervisor. It is helpful to ask what ways you might be able to improve. The supervisor may have suggestions or tips to help you do a better job. They may also be able to teach you new skills.

When a worker and supervisor understand each other, it makes the team stronger. This also is valuable when there is a problem. If two staff are fighting or a problem happens, you should try to work it out. This often means having the supervisor look into the situation. It is better to work out problems with assistance than to try to fix it alone.

I have seen many successful executives and have learned how they accomplish their goals. They certainly put their full efforts into their jobs. They also work outside of the company to learn to grow and become stronger. This includes gaining knowledge through magazines, books, self-help tapes and other ways to grow smarter.

We always want to be moving forward in our careers. We don't want to work at a job and not grow our skills. The many books and educational resources available will help you learn to become even more successful. It is clear that all of us have a greater potential and it is up to us to develop these abilities.

I want to finish this chapter talking about a very simple step. There are always different types of personalities within a job. You may find someone makes it harder to do your job. You may have valid reasons why their behavior is wrong. It is so powerful to learn to forgive and let go of anger. When you are upset, toxic emotions hold you back.

I remember working with a company where one of the staff seemed hostile. They were always late and had a poor attitude. This employee, named Kim, would try to find ways to get the boss in trouble by making up stories. This included trying to portray a situation that the boss didn't actually do. It reached a point where the other staff were upset and nervous working around Kim. The situation came to a head when Kim complained to the head of the business about the supervisor. This led to a detailed investigation of the accusations. They proved to be false and Kim admitted that she was having personal struggles. She was able to seek treatment and it led her co-workers to have empathy for her. They no longer looked at Kim as being mean and nasty. They came to understand that she was actually suffering and that it was extremely hard for her to do the job.

You may never know what your co-worker is facing. They may be having a tough time with their family, finances or health. When you choose to try and put yourself in their shoes, the anger dissipates. Many times, even those we are most angry at have a reason for their actions. This doesn't excuse negative behavior but this may help you continue to move forward.

I have seen workers learn to handle adversity and grow their own abilities. When they don't get upset and are able to work through problems they become stronger. It is never too much to ask for help if a problem is happening and you are not sure the best way to continue. You may find the answers and support you desire.

This is a section for you to answer. You can either do it on your own or with the group:

One way I could keep neater and better organized at work is:

If I am not sure what to do I will ask my supervisor because:

When I am helpful to other team members the benefit is:

If I am confused it is better to ask for help because:

It is better to let go of anger because it will help to:

I will always do my best because this teaches me to:

CHAPTER THREE

Healthy Choices

Does the way you live impact your potential success in your position? I share the story of Lisa to help you identify how your daily choices will contribute to higher levels of accomplishments. Lisa began a job working in sales for a large computer manufacturer. Her division was expected to call medium and large businesses to sell their companies. Each day she would make between 100-200 calls to develop new business.

The first few weeks were exciting and fulfilling. Lisa was enjoying making calls, had persistence and a positive attitude. The problem happened in her second month of work. She was not generating enough sales and became frustrated. In the evening, Lisa started to drink alcohol to help her handle her problems with work. This led her to struggle to wake up and arrive at the office on time. Lisa also failed to have the same enthusiasm each day. Her call numbers began to go down and her voice became weak. Her supervisor started to wonder if Lisa was a fit for the business. She was referred to me for counseling and I began to try and help her change her habits.

Lisa admitted that she loves working in sales. The problem was she started strong and then lost her positive attitude. She used alcohol as a way to numb her feelings and frustrations. We spoke how drinking would only harm her potential. I asked Lisa to identify ways that the alcohol was affecting her work performance. Lisa found that the drinking made her tired and hungover in the mornings. She also felt that her voice on the phone changed due to the alcohol from the night before.

We then decided to do an experiment. I asked Lisa what are five positive choices she could make daily. The list she came up with includes not drinking anymore, doing 30 minutes of physical exercise after work, listening to one self-help tape per week in her car, spending 20 minutes meditating in the morning and finally having a solid 7 hours of sleep each night before work. I was quite curious to see how her sales would change as she became healthier and happier.

The first shift was in Lisa's attitude. She was excited to wake up and work. Her mind and body was no longer tired because she was sleeping properly. Lisa started to believe that she could thrive in her job.

During the first week, potential clients were kind on the phone to her. She was connecting and started to obtain leads. Lisa closed two deals in her first week living a cleaner life. It also became obvious that Lisa finished each day feeling strong and healthy. She began to enjoy working out and feeling well rested. Within a few months, Lisa was thriving. Her numbers had improved to the top ten percent of the sales team. She improved her relationship with the other staff members and her supervisor.

Lisa has proven how our daily actions dictate our success. Many feel once they leave a place of employment they can handle themselves differently. When they are in the job, they follow the rules. Once they leave, they partake in negative behavior. The problem is that poor choices effect your productivity at work. There is a reason many athletes eat well, obtain enough sleep, attend long workouts and listen to positive influences. They understand that their actions will affect their performance.

I was providing therapy for Kevin, a supervisor who had been working on a loading dock at a newspaper for almost 40 years. He is usually helpful and kind to all of the staff he supervises. Kevin also relieves stress by doing daily outdoor walks and yoga. During the past few months, Kevin has stopped his after-work exercise.

There was one member on his team who was bothering him. This worker is often lazy, has an abrupt attitude and is irritating Kevin. One day, the worker, named Bill, was moving the daily papers slowly. Kevin became angry and started to scream at Bill. He told him that he was a waste of space and cursed at him. Even though Kevin had spent 40 years at the business, this was a problem. The union policies are that you cannot yell at an employee, especially in front of the other team members.

Kevin was mandated for therapy sessions with me. He felt horrible that he had lost his temper. Kevin came to accept that he needs healthy outlets outside of the workplace to handle the pressure and stress from his job. He made a point to apologize to Bill and is aware that his actions affected others. Kevin was able to go back to his job and is a very positive influence. We began to see even experienced workers could have problems if they don't keep mentally and physically strong. It is amazing to think that Kevin could have lost his job of 40 years for a 5 minute outburst of anger. The facts are anyone working in a business must try to do their best at all times. It is so helpful to find ways to properly deal with your emotions.

There are many simple ways to improve your abilities each day. The basics include sleeping well, eating healthy foods, doing physical workouts, reading educational books, listening to positive speakers, finding ways to stay calm and to have balance in your life. When you do these, you are given a chance to shine at work. Many of the most successful leaders have been able to see how their actions impact their work. You can start to develop your own abilities by taking care of your mind and body.

Please fill out these questions either as a group or on your own:

Why is it important to have enough sleep each night?

Why does drinking alcohol have the ability to harm your work performance?

List three steps you could take each day to take care of your mind and body.

What lessons did Lisa learn from her experience?

What was one lesson that Kevin was able to learn from the problem he faced at his job?

What is one major step you can make today to begin to improve your daily living?

CHAPTER FOUR

The Key Steps to Success

When you open up a door, there is often a key which properly fits the lock. If you do not have the right one, you will struggle to open the door. In our own lives, there are keys to success. You have the potential to find the right way to unlock you highest level of achievement.

I believe each of us have special gifts and abilities. We were created with unique talents, skills and minds. These tips will help you to understand how to break past road blocks. The four keys of success will work to expand your knowledge.

The first key is to learn what makes you tick. I was working with Hal who had been a Vice President at a local bank for 15 years. He was struggling to stay motivated and continue working. We discussed how his thoughts dictate his experience and reality. We made a list of the activities Hal enjoys as well as the parts of work that frustrate him.

The positive list was long and had many reasons why he enjoyed his job. They included the kind management that is always trying to find ways to help the staff grow and develop. Hal loved that the bank was always teaches that helping customers is the number one goal. He found supervising his team of 10 workers to be fun, challenging and always different. Hal also had developed many friendships during the last 15 years of work.

This is a solid list and proves why he had longevity in the job. We then started to speak about the negatives of his current work. The first was that he had a new manager who he reported to. The manager did not usually listen to Hal's ideas, even though many would be helpful. The manager also grew angry when Hal made a mistake. This made Hal nervous and uncomfortable. The last problem Hal had is the extended hours he had to complete each week. His new manager had changed his hours and now he worked Monday through Wednesday and then a full day on Saturday and Sunday. They were one of the only banks that offered hours both days of the weekend.

The keys for Hal to enjoy his work are to feel supported, appreciated and respected. He used to be able to openly communicate with his boss and discuss different issues. His new manager had a much different style and did not appreciate Hal's feedback. The new hours also are tough on Hal because he had children who were mostly around on the weekends. He missed seeing them and had been unable to attend their baseball and soccer games.

Hal and I began to discuss his options. He could either leave the job or continue to stay on board. He felt that the positives of the position still outweigh the negatives. I suggested he ask his boss for one weekly meeting where they could talk about the issues in the job. I also encouraged Hal to attend therapy, which would give him an outlet for any feelings or problems. The final step was to try and compromise. Hal knew he was needed on the weekends and that he must be there.

Hal and his sons began to start a Thursday ritual. He would pick them up from school and spend the whole evening with them on Thursday. Hal would also use Friday to take long hikes in his local nature park. He would also do errands and relax on his day off. These small changes were the key for Hal to begin to be happy again. He has lasted many additional years in his position.

The second key is to learn about your work process. Each of us handle learning and activities in different ways. When you master your own skills, you are more likely to see success. This takes practice and being open to know where you need to improve.

I began to help Chris after his supervisor encouraged him to seek help. Chris was very smart, creative and a talented sales executive. His problems were with his paperwork. The rules at his company were that each sales member must record who they call, comments about the discussion, additional notes and the next step. Chris was fantastic on the phone. His charming voice and kind manner led many potential clients to enjoy speaking with him. He would often close deals and had the gift of gab. The issues started to surface when his manager realized that Chris had not been using the note system.

When I spoke with Chris, he said that he has trouble staying organized. He also doesn't remember the details of each sales call. Chris is embarrassed to tell his boss he sometimes forgets the information. We came up with a strategy to improve Chris's performance.

He bought a notebook and for each call he would have a blank page. He would first write the name of the person and their information on the page. During the call, he would jot down notes on the paper. This would include all of the information he was supposed to enter in his work data sheets. When he completed a call, he would slowly transcribe the notes into the formal worksheet.

Chris also slowed down while making phone calls. He used to rush and just keep calling and this led to him being confused and forgetting a great amount of information. His new steady pace and more organized system helped him complete his job better. Within a month, his sales have grown and the supervisor is satisfied with his documentation.

Chris was scared to admit that he had certain problems before seeking help. When he found that his key to success was creating a system to stay organized it allowed him to progress. Many of us feel fear that our weak points should be hidden in a job. If you do not address your problems there are often issues that arise. This is why learning about your strengths and weaknesses is very helpful.

The third key to accomplishment is learning to relate with others. Many jobs have all types of workers with many different backgrounds. You may benefit from finding a way to get along with those on your team. It will help everyone involved when the staff is cooperative and connected.

I started to work with Deadra. She was working at a cosmetics company for the last four months. They make many high-end products including shampoos and perfumes. There is a factory where employees oversee the production of the products. Deadra works with eight other men and women to certify each product passes the safety test.

Deadra admitted to me that she is insecure. During her childhood, she was in foster care.

She was often bullied for being overweight and wearing old and worn clothes. This led her to not enjoy being around others. She had built a wall of defense mechanisms to handle her emotions. Deadra tried to be over confident to appear strong. During her job, many of the staff would talk together in the break room. They would share stories and have fun when they had a few minutes off from work. Deadra felt very uncomfortable during these breaks.

When one staff tried to be nice, Deadra started to seem too arrogant. She was new and her attitude led others to not enjoy being around her. This made Deadra sad and she started to miss work often. When we spoke, I realized that Deadra created her own problems from her childhood beliefs.

We began to find the authentic person Deadra actually was. It turned out under that pompous shell is a warm and loving person. She felt frightened to show her true self because she had been hurt before. With some intense sessions, Deadra decided to start being open and her experience at work shifted.

Within a short time, the staff responded differently to Deadra. They realized that she was warm and kind. They wanted to be her friend. They end up connecting with Deadra and were happy she was on their team. Deadra also felt excited to be making friendships at work. It had been many years since Deadra had nice co-workers to work with. She ended up being a very joyous and successful member of the team.

Deadra had to find the key to her own success. This meant learning how to overcome old problems and not bringing the baggage to her job. She worked on herself and realized that being kind was more rewarding. Her new attitude was the key to a successful career.

The final step to success is caring for those around you. Please know that everybody has feelings and emotions. You may not understand how your words and behaviors impact those you work with. It is vital to be kind to those who you see each day at your job.

I was helping Patty deal with the loss of her husband. He had died suddenly from a heart attack. They had been married for many years and it was an extremely hard time in Patty's life. She was feeling alone and upset. We began to work on helping her experience the different stages of grief. When she went back to work, she became very scared. She was nervous to be around others again. Patty didn't want to seem damaged and was fearful she would cry when thinking about the passing of her spouse.

Her team did something wonderful. When she was out, they each created a card to share how much Patty means to them. They also supported her during the difficult time. It was the first week back to her job and Patty was so happy. Patty said that it felt as though she had an additional family with her friends and co-workers. She believed that the kindness they had shown was helping her move on.

Patty also admitted that her relatives depended on her income even more now that she is widowed. If she was not able to return it would have created more stress and pressure. This was why one of the keys to success is helping those on your team.

You may never know how a smile, kind word or a helpful gesture will go towards improving the life of another human being. Many of us will go through a time where the support from our work team becomes vital to our future.

Please answer these questions either with your team or alone?

What did Hal learn that are his keys to success?

How did Chris change by learning to be more organized?

Did Deadra seeking therapy help her improve at her job? How did learning to get along with others help her?

How did Patty's co workers help her overcome a very tough loss?

What ways could you improve in your own position? What are your keys to doing better in your job?

CHAPTER FIVE

Seeking Help When You Need It

Does someone seem weak for needing help? Many feel fearful to ask questions and admit they do not know the answer. Many of the highest achievers were the ones who sought support and asked for advice. The President of The United States has a full team of advisors to help him learn, answer questions and give a well-rounded presentation for the many situations that arise. Many athletes have coaches, trainers and teammates that they confide in. Why do some workers feel scared to admit they need to ask for help?

I began to counsel Dave. He had been working at a company that manufactures a brand of nutritional bars. Dave grew up in a house where his dad always knew the answer. Even if his father was wrong, he would pretend to have everything under control . Dave mimicked the behaviors of his parent. He would never admit when he needed help.

This was working for a short time in Dave's job. When a mechanical error happened on a machine responsible for printing the wrappers, Dave was asked what went wrong. He made up a story and said he knew how to fix it. It turned out that Dave had no idea what happened and was unable to get the machine working again. He should have asked for help right away. Dave became embarrassed and didn't tell anyone about his inability to correct the problem.

Dave didn't tell his supervisor and the machine was out of commission for two days. This led to many products not being completed. It cost the company a large amount because Dave was scared to admit he made a mistake. His boss finally found out and Dave was in trouble. It took time but Dave started to see that it is better to be honest than to pretend you know how to handle something.

Dave confided in me that his low self-esteem interfered with him being honest. In his counseling, he learned that it actually takes more confidence to admit you need help. He began to slowly change and was no longer making poor decisions. He began to accept that when he didn't know something, he could ask his supervisor. It is better to seek help then to make a large mistake. This actually took a big weight off of Dave who tried to know everything and be perfect. He now can do the best he is able and seek help when he needs it.

I have also seen that many workers strive to cover up their errors. This may include denying or lying about a problem on the job. This usually leads to even more severe consequences and it is helpful to admit when a mistake has been made.

I was working with a girl who was at a large company that made toys. She began to take money from her business spending account and was using it for her own personal purchases. It started with one small item and she knew it was wrong. She said she didn't want to admit that she was doing this. She could have stopped and paid back the small amount she used. When she continued to spend money from her business account the situation became a major crime.

This woman went from making a small mistake to looking at a potential jail sentence. She could have easily admitted her error early on and stopped it from growing. Her failure to change and admit her mistake ended up creating a life-altering situation. Wouldn't it have been better if she was willing to face it in the beginning rather than let it become a huge issue with lawyers and many severe consequences?

Please know that your company does not expect you to know every single answer at all times. The best businesses are always working to teach their staffs. They have managers that are helpful and willing to answer questions. The team will work with you when you have made an error so you can quickly alleviate the problem.

What is the best way to ask a question? I encourage you to do so as soon as possible. When you do not know the answer, please speak with your supervisor. It is also helpful to ask your boss versus speaking with another member at your level. The reason is some coworkers may tell you to do it their way. If they are wrong, you are learning incorrect information. If your supervisor teaches you how to handle it, you are likely to achieve the outcome expected by your company.

One lesson is there are no dumb questions. Many worry that if they ask something simple they will sound stupid. This is not true. When you are not sure what the answer is it is better to seek help. I have seen how basic questions have the ability to help teams learn more. I am sure that most managers would want their staff to come to them when they are confused.

I was working with Luke who just began a position at a telemarketing company. Luke is very smart and always tries to work hard. During his two weeks of training, he was struggling to understand how to use the computer program.

He asked his trainer to walk him through how to enter data, change screens and save customer contact information. Luke was nervous he would appear incompetent if he asked for help. The training class had been going on for one week and this is one of the most important lessons. The instructor then asked the rest of the trainees if they also were confused. It turned out that almost every person had the same question! If Luke had not asked it would have hurt his co-workers and created serious problems.

The supervisor told Luke he had done the right thing. There were several other questions asked that day, all because Luke was willing to ask what he did not know. Many finally had the courage to seek help. They became a stronger group because each member felt able to learn and be honest about what they do not know.

Please answer these questions with the group or alone:

What are the benefits of asking a question when you are not sure about something?

Why is it better to be honest about something when you make a mistake?

When you don't know something, why is it best to ask your supervisor?

What have you learned about the importance of asking questions?

The Positive Worker

CHAPTER SIX

Your Best Effort Daily

Each day is a new beginning. You may start each day feeling positive, friendly, hopeful, helpful and ready to enjoy work. The worker who places the most amount of effort into their job often obtains the most success. I have had the honor of meeting many who accomplished the highest levels of business success. The one common ingredient was they always tried their hardest.

I met a CEO, named Jose, of a large business in New York. He shared how he moved to this country and barely spoke the language. Jose started working in a factory and worked very hard. He used some of his wages to take classes to learn English. Each day, he was the most attentive, hardest working and most helpful factory worker.

Within a few months, he was given a raise of 50 cents. In his new position, he tried even harder. Each morning, he was helpful and always was willing to put in his best efforts. Over the next ten years, he continued to rise higher professionally. Jose went from barely speaking English to being a manager of a department supervising fifty workers.

Jose spent much of his off hours studying business. He would go to his local library and read books about business leadership. He learned about the lives of Andrew Carnegie, Thomas Edison, Henry Ford and any others who achieved success. Jose would also borrow books on tape in both English and Spanish. He was now fluent in English.

Jose was always offering to take on extra work and help his company. The President of the business began to take notice of Jose's efforts. They decided to make him a Vice President of a large division. Jose didn't stop working hard. He came to the office with a smile, a great outlook and began to mentor other workers. Jose felt grateful to the business and all of the accomplishments they allowed him to work on. He now had a home and lived abundantly.

It was 25 years since Jose began working as a low paid employee in the factory of this business. The CEO wanted to retire and needed a replacement. Jose was his first choice to take his place. Jose became the first Latin American employee ever made CEO of a company this large. He has helped the business continue to grow and accomplish even larger tasks. Jose now runs a charity helping others who come to our country looking for a better life.

He does speeches in many communities to teach his lessons about the benefit of hard work. Jose shares how his positive attitude, determination and consistency led to a large amount of success. Jose still comes to work smiling and helping each person he encounters.

There are many examples of leaders who began doing their best exactly where they are placed. They end up proving their commitment while moving up within their company. The impact of hard work and consistent effort is often rewarded with even more achievement.

You may wonder how to do your best each day. One step is to be kind to everyone you encounter. Each person is important and deserves kindness and respect. This creates a business where each member feels valued and supported.

One other step is to do more than you are expected at work. If the goal is to make 20 sales calls, how about making 30? If your boss asks you to clean your workspace once a week, how about doing it every day? These may seem like minor differences, but they will impact your work performance.

I met a top producer at a business that sold financial products. His name was Michael and I asked how he became number 1 out of over 2,000 financial advisers. He told me that when he was training he was supposed to work from 8 a.m. to 4 p.m. He would wake up at 4:30 a.m. and arrive at work at 6 a.m. During the extra hours, he would study, practice his pitch and connect with his boss.

Michael then said he was expected to make 100 calls per day. He would consistently work late and usually called around 200 per day. When he began to obtain clients, he placed extra effort in helping them. He was available 7 days a week to answer their questions. He also created a database of their favorite movies, birthdays, anniversaries, restaurants, and other events. Michael would send them a beautiful handwritten card on each of their major life events. He also studied and remembered all of the important pieces of their lives so he could be connected to his clients. They felt as if he was a friend because he always kept in touch and was invested in their well-being.

Michael achieved lots of success in his company, but continued to work hard. He now runs a team. He spends a few hours each day calling his long list of clients. It is often to help them, listen to their situations and stay a part of their lives. He now mentors many others workers with a goal of helping them reach their full potential. Michael knows caring about others is one of the most important ways to grow.

The final part of Michael's work is to continue growing mentally. He reads a new book each week and is part of several networking groups. Michael is always wanting to expand his knowledge and become an even better team member. His lessons for success are well rooted in why hard work and great effort leads to accomplishment.

You may feel that your job is basic. It is in your power to always work at the highest possible level. What are ways you may grow stronger and obtain even more knowledge? It may mean coming to work each day with the best possible outlook. You may ask your boss what lessons they have learned that have helped them succeed.

Professional Athletes are a great example in learning work ethic. They have accepted that the more effort you place in training, the better chance you have of success. You may also find that the hardest working teams win in their chosen fields. Do you want your company to grow and expand?

The final piece of your daily work is learning to never give up. You may have hit some type of wall that feels tough. If you are in sales, you may be in a slump. If you are in design, there may be a creative block. When you make that next call with excitement, attentiveness and warmth it may lead to a new customer. Many have overcome tough slumps by being willing to keep a great attitude.

Mary is a strong worker. She sells phone systems to businesses. The economy has been slowing and her team's numbers are very low. Many are fearing that they are going to lose their jobs. Mary decided she would try even harder. She went from 60 calls daily to over 120. She also encouraged her coworkers to place the higher level of effort.

Her first two months led her to be the top sales person. It became clear that her extra effort was helping. This led many other sales members to do the same. Within four months, the team was well over their quota. They had worked together to achieve success. It all started with Mary being willing to try harder and keep a great attitude. Her persistence and skill led her whole company to grow. Is it possible that one person trying harder can impact a huge company?

The answer is that you make a big difference. The way you work and the efforts you place can make a dramatic difference. Each person has a major role to play within a business. When you come into the office each day with optimism it has an impact. You will find that staying calm, kind, hardworking, passionate, persistent and helpful will allow your team to win in the business world.

Please answer these questions either as a group or individually:

Why is it important to try your hardest each day at work?

What were some of the reasons Jose went from an entry-level job to the CEO of his company?

What were some of the reasons Michael achieved success?

Mary made a major difference at her job. What did she do that helped the company achieve their sales numbers?

What are three benefits of being optimistic, persistent, kind and helpful at your job?

CHAPTER SEVEN

The Best Teams Work Together

Each day, work teams come together to achieve goals. This may include creating products, selling services or innovating to develop new technologies. Many ask what the importance of teamwork is within different corporations. The best answer is that even the best player loses the game when their team fails.

It is easy to understand the game of baseball. Each team member individually bats with the goal of scoring runs. When one player hits a homerun, the team is doing well. If the rest of the team is unable to score points or stop the opponent from scoring, they will lose. You cannot win a championship without your team working together.

I was early in my social work career when I began to see the power of teamwork. One of my earliest clients was a man named Maury. He had taken over a family business that created beautiful art sold in major retailers. His grandfather and father worked most of their lives to establish this business. Maury was in his mid-thirties when his father became ill.

Maury took over the business. The first problem was that many of the staff were upset about his dad being ill. They were concerned about the business and loved working for his dad. They also were nervous that many staff could be let go if the ownership changed.

I started to share with Maury that he would improve his business by connecting with his team. He started a daily morning breakfast for the 50 staff members. He provided bagels from the best local store in their suburban town. He tried to talk to every employee and create more openness. The team started to see that Maury has many of the favorable characteristics that allowed his dad to be a great leader.

The second step was that Maury instituted an open door policy. This meant if any type of problem or question arose during the day, he was available to offer help. The team thought this was a wonderful way to open up communication. It was a great tool that gave Maury even more insight into the different challenges as they appear.

The last step was to build morale. Maury started a softball team that played twice a week. He covered the costs for uniforms and equipment. The workers love playing together and having fun outside of the office. These different simple steps created a team atmosphere at work. The staff started to again work together and help improve the business. The creative team was able to thrive and make innovative new products. The sales staff were better at their selling and hit higher targets. The administrative workers had a new enthusiasm and an improved outlook. This is how Maury helped his team to win.

The hardest part of being on a team is to find your own important place. This is best illustrated when we look at the Chicago Bulls during the years when Michael Jordan was on their team. Many know that Michael is possibly the greatest basketball player in the history of the game. He could not win without the team that would support him. Many of the other team members had to know their role. They would feed the ball to Michael often and also do their best on defense. The coaches would work to teach the team how to handle the opposing players and limit their scoring.

When the team came together they would often win many games. It is important to know that you don't have to be the number one scorer to be a valuable asset to your team. You may be in administration but your work keeps the business going. If you are in sales, your clients help generate revenue for your company. The staff that cleans the bathrooms and desks does an important job creating a clean place for everyone to work.

Why should every team member feel valued? When we know that our work is important there is a higher chance we will put in our full efforts. I was once coaching a client who posed a very interesting question. His name was Troy and he said, "Is everyone supposed to become a CEO, high-level executive or owner of a business?"

I began to think about what he was asking. Many of the books and motivational lectures teach how you have the ability to rise to the highest level. There is often the idea that you could become the owner of your own business or the boss of another company. It took a few moments but then the answer became clear.

I told Troy that many of us do have the potential to rise higher in our lives. There is also a place for each person in our world. I said, "Troy, what would happen if every human being was the CEO of a business? Who would work in sales, file the paperwork, handle the accounting, clean the office, handle human resources and design the service and products? Why are there so many humans beings that look and are different? Why are we all born within different gifts and abilities?"

Troy and I continued to speak about this very valid topic. Troy grew to understand that his goal was to find his own unique purpose. It reinforced that most of us have different abilities and it is up to us to try and grow our own strengths. There is no member of a team that is less valuable than another. You should take pride knowing that the work you are doing makes a difference in the business you are working in.

There are four tips that teach about teamwork. The first is to understand your own strengths and weaknesses. You are able to be a better team member when you know what needs to be improved. You may ask your boss or coworkers to help you develop the pieces of your abilities that need strengthening.

The second tip is to assist those around you. When you notice that your teammate looks confused ask them if they need help. If you see someone on your team who appears upset, you could ask them if they want to talk about what they are feeling. When your boss asks for someone to help them with a task, it is wonderful to be the one to volunteer. When a worker is out sick, you may step up to help with the work they are unable to do while absent.

The third step is to find a way to connect with those around you. It may be as simple as saying hello or asking how their day is going. When you start to be friendly to your team it helps everyone involved. There are many who love going to work because they feel supported and enjoy the staff they work with.

The final step to being a great team member is being willing to adapt to change. When a new procedure or idea is taught, you are open to adjustments. If you maintain a positive attitude it takes the pressure off of your supervisor. It also encourages the rest of the team to follow your lead of being cooperative.

Please answer these questions either as a team or individually:

What are three steps Maury took to help improve his company?

Why was every member of The Chicago Bulls important to their team?

What are the lessons Troy learned about?

What are the four tips for teamwork and why they are important?

CHAPTER EIGHT

Shifting Your Attitude

The way we see the world is our choice. When we wake up each morning, it is a decision to Say, "What a wonderful day," or, "Oh, no, I have to get up and go to work." Many of us learn to find reasons to be unhappy. It may be that a parent was always negative. You may have made friends that live in misery, sharing about how horrible everything is going.

You have the ability to make your own life better. I want to share my own personal journey and how shifting my thoughts turned around my life. I grew up with a dad that was often negative. He would share how many problems and issues were happening in our world. I started my life copying his negative outlook. I began to see that I would not always try my hardest because being pessimistic created doubt in my mind. If something wasn't going well, I would often give up.

When I grew up, I began to attend therapy and learn that we control our own thinking. I began to spend a great amount of time studying optimism. I would read, listen and focus on positive thoughts. I began to say affirmations to myself each day. Within a few years, I completely turned around my thinking pattern. I would go on to help thousands also change their negative habits and learn to be happier.

I began to work with Stephanie. She was raised with two parents that were always fighting and complaining. They hated their jobs, battled money problems, and thought life wasn't fair. Stephanie took a job after high school and hated it. She began to complain and was let go from the position. She started working with me and I had trouble helping her break free from her negativity.

It became clear that Stephanie wanted to change her outlook life. She began to study optimism. Stephanie began to read self-help books that share how to develop a healthier outlook. Stephanie also listened to motivational speakers while driving in her car. Each morning

Stephanie said affirmations that trained her to be more optimistic.

Stephanie began a new job. It was the first time in her life that she felt excited to work. She started the job and was kind to everyone. She placed her full effort and positive energy into the tasks at her job. She found new friends and was having fun while feeling more alive.

Stephanie would eventually be given a raise and see herself rise within the company. Her outlook and mindset shifted everything in her life. She would become a happy and friendly person. She said it felt so much easier to be positive than to live in negativity. Stephanie admitted that she used to be miserable almost all of her life. When she learned to change her thinking, she was able to make the best of everything she encountered.

There is a question that we all must look at. Do you want to be positive? If you spend much of your time focusing on your problems and what is wrong does it make you feel happy? Does being pessimistic help achieve more or does it obstruct your potential?

We can talk ourselves out of anything. You may have a great job, but being negative will attract problems. A sales executive may be able to close deals but being a pessimist may stop a buyer from moving forward. Why are many of the most successful business owners optimistic? It is because staying positive is a key ingredient for business success.

I started to work with Robert to help him improve his attitude. He was scared to be positive because he thought there was no reason to focus on optimism. Robert asked, "If I am positive, will it take away all my problems and make everything go perfectly?" I smiled and told him that this was an awesome question.

I looked at Robert and agreed being happy does not take away issues. What it does is allow you to overcome the problems that arise in your life. When a company starts to sell a product and people are not buying, there are a few options. One is to be negative and give up. They can stop selling, close the business and say it is a failure. The other choice is to try a different tactic to selling the product. They may also begin to brainstorm new offerings that may sell better than this one. It is possible they will pivot and take what they have learned to create something that delivers greater profitability.

There are many examples of business leaders who fail only to come back stronger than before. When Steve Jobs was fired from Apple, did he give up on achieving his goals? He went and started another business that eventually was bought by Apple and he was asked to come back and be the new boss. When Thomas Edison failed thousands of times to invent his version of the lightbulb did he quit or grow negative? Edison kept persisting and eventually brought his invention to light our world.

We each have reasons to be positive or negative. You will become more successful by teaching your brain to find an encouraging thought. This does not mean you have to walk around smiling all day long. It takes time to change your thought pattern. It will help your life to develop a better outlook.

I am helping a man named Owen learn to improve his thinking pattern. Owen is usually kind and warm but he is feeling sad because his dad passed away. Owen shared that the loss is leading him to be negative about life. It impacts his job and he wants to change his feelings.

We began to speak about his life. Owen shared that his dad was one of his greatest teachers. He is upset that he will no longer be around. It is a very hard fact to know that his father will no longer be there to support and help him grow.

Owen slowly started to feel better. He began every morning saying the following affirmations to himself, "I am happy to be alive another day. I am going to enjoy today and have fun. I am happy to be able to work and be productive. My life keeps getting better." It began to work within a few weeks. Owen started to feel alive and found his joy.

It also was important that Owen go back to the gym. He ran and lifted weights for an hour in the evening after his work was finished. This led to Owen feeling stronger and having an outlet for his energy. It was not long before Owen was enjoying his life. He even admitted that he is more joyful now that he was a few years ago. Owen knows enjoying his life is the best

way to honor his fathers memory.

Please answer these questions with the group or alone:

How did optimism help Stephanie improve her situation?

How did persistence help Thomas Edison?

What were two steps Owen took to improve his life?

What could you do to help yourself learn to be more positive?

CHAPTER NINE

Setting Personal and Team Goals

There are many ways that having goals keeps us moving forward. It starts to clarify what we are working to accomplish. It is also a gauge to see how closely we are able to achieve our targets. There are several ways that proper goal setting allows us to grow stronger.

When I was young, I met several entrepreneurs who have built big businesses. I was very curious to find out if there was a recipe for how they accomplished their success. I was shocked when they all stated that they had a plan and worked toward making this happen. I wanted to look deeper in understanding the benefit of planning and working towards goals.

My father worked selling products that were sold in retailers during the holiday season. He shared with me that stores are often planning and buying for their stores as early as two years before they sell products. This was fascinating and sometimes, during Christmas, stores were buying products for summer, the following Christmas and even years beyond this. They had to try to analyze what products would be selling, and how many orders to place and what sales to offer.

How would they know what people would buy well before it is the time to buy? They would create figures and estimates using the knowledge and skills that they have developed over many years. It is possible they would make a mistake but it is vital to plan.

I have seen how employees learn to achieve great tasks by creating obtainable personal goals. I was helping a salesman named Thomas who worked in a retail store. He was earning around $12.00 per hour and wanted to one day become a manager. We spoke about ways he could contribute more to his company and help move forward. I asked if there were sales quotas in his department at the store. Thomas said they did have goals for the whole store but that each employee did not have a personal goal.

Thomas and I came up with an idea for him to improve his sales goals. He set personal goals of trying to work hard to help customers, improve the whole stores' sales and be recognized for his extra efforts. Thomas began to ask his managers if there were any ways he could help improve the sales or improve customer relations. Thomas was told that he could walk the floor of the store and offer assistance to anyone who might need it. He began to help many clients and personally show them the items they were looking for.

The next step was for Thomas to show his leadership. He began to show the other store workers how he helps assist customers. Thomas also had begun to lead a group discussion called "How We Help Customers." The sales staff had begun to study self-help books, interact more with their customers and keep a positive attitude. The results have been phenomenal.

The store became number one in sales out of the 30 locations they have in the South. When the high-level managers were asked why the numbers improved, the store shared about Thomas. They spoke how he has been helping set goals and improve the team. It was not long before Thomas was made an assistant manager. His extra effort and goals helped to improve his store. This led to him moving up and being seen as an effective manager.

Please do not ever feel that your goals are not important. When you clean the office with a high level of effort, it impacts the environment. When a customer goes into the bathroom and finds it neat and clean, they feel happier about the location. In a retail environment, having all the items stocked properly makes customers feel that the store works hard to be organized. When a worker is extra helpful and accommodating, the customers will continue to shop and want to be a client.

How do we set simple goals? The easiest are the ones you are in power of working on. This includes showing up to work every day, both on time and prepared to work. You also should have a goal of having a positive attitude and being helpful to everyone on your team. The next goal is to put in your full effort each day at work. When you are lazy or waste time you are losing an opportunity to see success. You should come to work with your clothes clean, have pride in your appearance and be ready to work. This includes having slept enough the night before, being alert and preparing to provide your best efforts.

The team you work on will also have suggestions of other goals. You may ask your manager or supervisor what goals they believe you should work on and develop. One might be to put more effort in an area that you could use improvement. It may also be a goal within your company that everyone is working on. When you choose to ask what type of goals you can set and achieve, you are demonstrating leadership. You're showing your boss that you take your work seriously. This will lead to them having more confidence in your work and also seeing you in a positive light.

Each of us are responsible for our own actions. When you are part of a team, everyone has a goal in mind. I began to work with a young man named Hector. He was working for an office that sold outdoor furniture at a retail location. Hector was asked to come for therapy because he was missing work often and was found napping several times during the day. My first question to Hector was if he wanted the job. His response was terrific.

Hector said of course he wanted the job and he actually needed it. He would not waste his time in therapy if he didn't want to maintain his position. I then asked why his behavior was poor and he was sleeping during work. Hector admitted that he did take a few naps each day. He told me that his mother was ill and he had been caring for her at night. Hector had to wake up and bring her water and help her go to the bathroom frequently at night. This was a valid reason for why he was so sleepy during the work day.

I began to ask Hector if there were any other options. I told him that sometimes nurses are able to come in and help elderly individuals who are sick. If she has state insurance, this service is sometimes covered to the patient at no cost. He looked into it and found that a nurse could come at night to help his mother. This allowed Hector to set some new goals.

Hector had three main goals. One is to show up each day on time to his job. The second is to sleep enough at night so he would not be tired during his work time. The third step was to show extra initiative by hitting his highest personal sales for the months of October, November and December. He began to work on all three goals. It took extra effort but it began to take shape.

His first full month back was a huge success. Hector was on time every day and did not fall asleep once during the work shifts. He also was placing a large amount of effort helping shoppers and closing sales. He was the third highest in sales for his team for the month of October. He began to see how positive his boss was handling his new attitude and efforts. Hector continued to work on new goals and be a positive worker. He began to learn how planning and working towards a goal was able to improve his life. Hector decided that therapy was actually a wonderful way for him to grow and change. He completed our sessions and was very happy that he learned new ways of living.

I began to learn that each of us have a higher potential. You may be the CEO of your business but there are new goals to obtain. When you begin to look at how to grow, it develops your skills. It also shows the work and efforts you may place into your daily tasks. These days, work is extremely important to everyone involved. When an employee is striving, growing, learning and listening they place a vital piece in making progress. The best businesses will fail when their staff do not keep placing effort into their jobs. Isn't it better to be self-motivated than to only do things because you are fearful of being fired? Your job is a reflection on your life. When you do the work with warmth, kindness, effort and persistence it says a great deal about your own ways of living. It is up to you to have the willingness to learn, grow and develop your goals.

Please answer these questions either as a group or alone:

What goals did Thomas have?

What are some simple goals you can set?

How did Hector change after he had a nurse help his mother?

Is your job a reflection on your life? Why should you take your work and job seriously?

CHAPTER TEN

Keeping Yourself Physically Strong

The effort we place in keeping physically strong has a key component in our ability to work. When we feel healthy, strong, active and alive most of our days are happier. It all begins in remembering the rewards for taking care of yourself.

I was helping Leticia after she came to work on her career and life. Leticia was struggling to balance being a mom, working at a restaurant and caring for herself. She was about 30 pounds overweight and always feeling tired. I started learning about her life and trying to understand where her problems were coming from.

One of the best questions I asked was if she spent a great amount of her time on herself. Leticia was often discussing trying to help her children, working to keep her customers happy and assisting her friends. She became extremely sad when I asked about her own self-care. Leticia started to cry when she said she always puts herself last. This was the door opening to starting to see self-changes.

We had several discussions about why it is important for Leticia to take care of herself. Many of the best caretakers forget to help themselves while focusing on others in need. This leads to many negative consequences that may impact both your work and health. Leticia began to identify that there are many reasons to nurture her mind and body.

She started to carve out time to do a 30 minute workout 4 days a week. She would walk on a treadmill in the free gym at her neighborhood center. This would help her to stay fit and lose some of the extra pounds. It also helped to increase her energy. Leticia began to see many positive changes in her life.

The efforts of working out in the gym allowed her to have less stress. She was more patient with her children and was able to handle watching them. Leticia found that she was doing better at her job. She was being more understanding of her customers' needs and also having improved interactions with the other employees. It was also fascinating that she was less tired and had been having enough energy to handle her responsibilities.

The facts are that each of us have the potential to use physical activity to stay strong. I was once asked how to help someone that has an illness or trouble walking. The answer is that even stretching, walking slowly, moving yourself or any activity is helpful. Each of us are at different levels and abilities in terms of exercise. I also have witnessed how some are very tired and out of shape when they begin a workout regimen.

David is a 45 year old man that works selling insurance. The majority of his work is selling through the phone. He is employed at a large insurance company with a room of employees selling to new potential customers. It is a long day and he is on the phones from 9 a.m. until 6 p.m.

He began to smoke cigarettes during college. David is given 4-5 breaks each day where he goes out of the office to have a cigarette. He speaks with other coworkers that smoke and enjoys this brief time leaving his office. The problem began when the nicotine addiction led his health to deteriorate. David began to have nosebleeds and sore throats that was harming his ability to work.

David spoke to his primary care physician who confirmed that his health problems are from his smoking habit. The doctor began to advise changes for him to improve his life. This would begin with quitting smoking, beginning to slowly do physical activity and eat healthier foods. David was reluctant to make these changes but he knew both his life and job were on the line.

I started to help David learn the psychological reasons for his behaviors. He admitted that he has become lazy and has been uninterested in changing. It was a wake-up call that he now believes he must deal with. We start to talk about jogging and David says he becomes winded due to his smoking. We came up with a plan for him to walk 20 minutes a day for 5 days each week.

David was able to do this and felt better after his walks. He used a patch to help him give up smoking. It was very hard but he fought his way through quitting smoking. David also found a local healthy supermarket and he picked better quality food. This combined to help him feel stronger. It was not long before his walks doubled in time and distance. He also found that his breathing was calmer and his health was improving.

One year later, David has continued to make positive progress. He is now running 45 minutes a day for 6 days a week. He feels happier and his breathing is stronger. His job is also seeing the benefits of his physical efforts. David is obtaining more new customers and has earned the most money he has ever made. The reason for his success is that David understands that his physical and mental health impact all aspects of his life.

When you focus on improving your health the first person to benefit is you. It will not be long before other areas of your life also are being changed. One of the biggest secrets of successful people is learning that their best investment is in themselves. When they eat well, workout and take care of their body it impacts their work. You will grow your abilities when you live in a healthy manner. One of the biggest costs to companies is having workers be sick, not doing their best and making errors. Your physical health plays a major role in each of these situations. You will help your business and your own life by making the choice to develop healthy habits.

There are some easy ways to begin improving your physical health today. You can draft a chart that will detail all of the activities you are going to do for the next week. You may ride a bike, take a hike, jog in your neighborhood, do stretching, take a yoga class, dance, play basketball or any other activity. When you keep track of this you will learn accountability. You may also feel the accomplishment of seeing yourself improve your health.

I want to share my own story that has allowed me to improve my physical abilities. I had gained over 40 pounds and was not doing much exercise. My choice of foods were often chips, pizza and other fast foods. I was only in my twenties and began to feel tired and slow. It also became clear that my moods were impacted from these negative habits. I didn't like going to the gym and felt that each time I went it was a struggle. One day, I made a choice to change my ways.

I began to go each day at 4 p.m. for a walk in my neighborhood. I started with 25-30 minutes each day. The first week was hard but I was determined to stick with it. I continued doing this five days a week for several months. I began to lose weight and feel happier. I then extended my efforts to a 45 minute walk each day. Within one year, I was up to one hour and was coming back to life. I was also eating better foods and starting to feel more joyful.

This blossomed into a love of physical pursuits. I began to feel strong enough to hike very large mountains. I also am able to play basketball and enjoy running up and down the courts. One of my favorite activities is going to my local nature park. I do an intense workout of walking, running, squatting, push ups, dips and other intense activities. I have lost all of the weight that had been holding me back. I began to see my writing, coaching, and helping others had improved. I share these lessons because they have changed my own life.

It may seem as if you are too far to become healthy. I had to go slow and do what I was capable of in the beginning. When you make small and consistent changes, it leads to long-term success. You should make a choice to improve your health today. Your mind and body will be thankful for the efforts you place in caring for yourself.

Please answer these questions either as a group or on your own:

Why does Leticia need to focus on taking care of herself?

What did David's doctor suggest he do to improve his health?

What are the benefits of the changes David made?

The author shared his own story. What did he do to improve his health?

What are a few ways you could begin to be physically healthier?

CHAPTER ELEVEN

Practice Makes Positivity

We learn many of our lessons through repetition. A basketball player becomes skillful by taking thousands of continued shots at the basket. A tennis player learns to serve by practicing thousands of attempts. A great salesperson becomes a success by continuing to master the art of selling. The same lesson is easily applicable to learning to be positive.

I began to work with a company and their team. They were open that one worker always seemed to be angry and focusing on the negative. His name was Trent and he did not want to be in this team-building session. I began to ask Trent why he felt this was not important. Trent did not hold anything back and began his discussion. He said no training would change his team. The fighting was because everyone had been disrespecting him and making him feel like an outcast. Trent was nasty to his team because they were mean towards him. Trent finished by saying they did a team-building class once before and things ended up even worse than they were prior to the class.

It was clear that Trent did not want to be here. He had no belief that any of this would help him. He also was holding onto anger from the many problems that had been facing the company. I asked Trent if he would attempt to follow some of my lessons for one week. If nothing changed, I would agree to leave and end the team training. If things were improving, Trent must commit to the full month of team building. His eyes lit up and he said, "You got a deal, my man!"

The first lesson was that Trent would wake up in the morning saying five positive things. This would include the following: I am going to improve my relationships with my workers. I am appreciated and respected at my job. I help others and they help me. I will show up on time and put in my full efforts. My job is a fun and enjoyable part of my life. Trent promised to say these each morning before coming to work.

The second lesson was for Trent to show gratitude to his team. This included him buying bagels one morning for each of his co-workers. He would tell each one a positive reason he is happy to be on their team. Trent was confused but he proceeded to follow this step.

The third step was for Trent to listen. He would let his co-workers speak and not answer until they were done with their thought. This was one of the major problems his team had with him. He would often only listen for a moment and then focus on what he was interested in doing. This led many to feel as though he didn't care about them.

These steps were all done and the team validated that Trent had accomplished these. I sat with the team and asked Trent how this all worked out. His answer sheepishly was, "You're right coach. I changed my ways and then everybody treated me different. Maybe some of the problems were coming from my actions. I accept I need to work on myself if I want my team to treat me right."

Over the next few weeks, Trent continued to change his attitude and behaviors. His team also worked on the reasons the fighting had been happening. Within a short time, they were coming together and helping each other. They went from hating each other to finding reasons they could work together. It was not long before these positive changes led to a better business. It all started with practicing and being willing to change your ways.

The art of persistence has the ability to make anything happen. You may begin to identify how you could become more positive. This might mean listening more, finding ways to be helpful, having an optimistic outlook and treating others with warmth. This may not be your natural way of being but you can learn to change.

Do we have the ability to do things differently? If you knew your life depended on smiling, helping and being kind would you able to do this? The answer is of course you could accomplish being more positive. You may ask the simple question of what is in it for you if you learn to be more positive? There often should be a valid reason why you work on something.

Would you buy a product from someone who is smiling, complimenting you, trying to cheer you up, laughing and has a warm attitude? Would you buy something from someone who is nasty, complaining, making you feel bad and focusing on everything that is wrong? The answer is most human beings enjoy being around others who are positive. When you are around a negative person it brings you down and takes away your joy. It will also harm your job and environment.

When you practice positivity, you are developing a winner's outlook. Most of the great successes in life are those who kept a wonderful outlook. They do not let problems or issues stop them from continuing their efforts. They persist and are always finding the silver lining in life. What do you feel when you meet someone who is warm, kind and helpful? When you are having a bad day, do you want someone to agree that everything is horrible or be around the person who motivates and lifts your spirit?

There is always a way to develop your strengths. I suggest listening to and reading self-help books. There are wonderful books and audio tapes that teach lessons. You can find ones that support your growing happier and healthier. There is also a valid reason to seek assistance if you are struggling. Many go through periods of times that it feels hard to be positive. You may have ended a relationship, lost a loved one or feel financially strapped. These are strong issues that may make you upset.

There are always therapists in your area to help you work on your life. It may make sense to seek the support of a trained expert. They can give you an outlet for the problems and issues you are facing. I often let my clients vent when they have heavy issues on their minds. I have learned that it is better to let our emotions out than to hold on to heavy feelings. The difference is that therapists are professionally trained to help others deal with their feelings.

When someone complains in my office I am not harmed in the least. I know how to listen and help them work through their thoughts. This is what a therapist is capable of doing. When you complain to your boss and co-workers, it will lead to a different interaction. If you are spending a large amount of time telling everyone what is wrong you will begin to be looked at in a negative manner. It is up to you to choose to come to work and to leave your baggage at home. You are not in a job for the company to handle your problems. You are expected to take care of yourself and seek outside help if you are mentally or emotionally struggling. The best workers know that seeking therapy for their problems is a healthier and wiser choice. You then learn how to overcome your issues with a professional who is prepared to help you. Your teammates are there to work and not be your therapist. Please know the difference.

There are many who are positive today that used to be unhappy. I want to share about a few workers that wake up each day with a smile and are as kind as you could imagine. Saul is always friendly and one of the most helpful workers. You might not know that he was once a drug addict who spent time in prison. Karly is a fantastic sales executive. She is one of the warmest and friendliest members of her team. You would not be able to tell that both of her parents died in a car crash 12 years ago. Emily is one of the greatest executive assistants. She is poised, extra friendly and well loved by all of her team. You would not know that Emily was homeless eight years ago after dealing with an abusive boyfriend.

I share these stories because optimists are not perfect people. They have not always had all of their lives as a walk in the park. Many of us have faced immense struggles. The difference is we have been willing to seek help and handle our issues. We then find the courage to press forward and keep a positive outlook. Would you know from reading this book that my only brother died suddenly from a drug overdose at age 27 one year ago? Would you know that I once faced an illness that nearly ended my life? You would not because I have learned to handle my problems and still keep going with a wonderful outlook. It is not the situations that we encounter in our lives that determine our happiness. It is our choice in how we decide to handle the issues as they arise. Your strength will come from finding a way to stay positive no matter what changes you encounter.

Please answer these questions either with the group or alone:

How did Trent change? What did he do differently and what was the result?

Do we have the ability to do things differently? How can we change?

What did Saul and Emily face?

What are ways you can work to be more positive?

How does staying positive help workers find success?

CHAPTER TWELVE

Learning to Connect With Co Workers

When you work in an office there will be many others to interact with. You will find that navigating different personalities helps you have a more positive outlook. The reality is many of us are able to grow our ability to connect with different types of people.

I began to work with Betty after she was dealing with some hard emotions. She had been working in sales for about eight years. She was very determined and persistent with her job. Over the past year, she had been having major problems at work. I began to ask her what the issues were that had been making her job difficult.

Betty began to open up that the company has about 40 male sales executives and about 8 women. Betty was always able to get along with the men but had been having major issues relating to the other female staff. The other women felt that she was cold towards them and that she did not put effort into improving their relationship. They cited examples that two of the women had birthday parties and invited the whole team to attend. Betty did not go to either. What made the women angry was that Betty had attended all the male staffs birthday parties.

I started to ask Betty if she liked the other women at work. She said that she felt uncomfortable around women. This went back to her childhood and the relationship she had with her mom. Her mother was extremely critical towards Betty. Her mom would put down the clothes she wore, her hair, makeup and her weight. Betty admitted that her mom's actions have made her insecure and to have a negative attitude about women. Betty even admitted that she had almost no female friends, which had been something she wanted to change.

Betty and I began to discuss this very important problem. I asked Betty if she was giving the women at her work a solid attempt. They had been nice enough to invite her to birthday parties. The other woman were making an effort and it seemed that Betty was rejecting them. I also asked Betty if it was fair to punish other women for the actions of her mom. Do the women she works with have any power to change what her mom did so long ago? Betty began to cry and open up about her heavy feelings.

She began to accept that her issues had been there for a long time. We devised a plan to help her connected with the women at her job The first part of the process was to apologize. She would tell the women she was sorry she didn't attend their parties. Betty would also invite them out to lunch and see if they were willing to start a friendship. Many of them agreed to go with her and this began a long process of connecting them. Betty found that the effort helped her feel happier at work and filled a void that was created long ago by her mother. She now sees that she can enjoy all types of co-workers and be a better member of her work team.

Why do some of us enjoy being alone rather than in groups? I have found that many human beings are extremely sensitive. When someone calls us a name, hurts our feelings or frustrates us it is very difficult. There are some who socially shake off any of these experiences and just keep going. When you are very sensitive, you may feel too vulnerable to handle the experience of being hurt by others.

The issue is that we all must learn to be able to get along with each other. When you are in a work setting there are likely different staff you must engage with. One clear way to change is to grow your own self confidence. When you view yourself in a positive manner, it helps you not focus on what others think of you.

I began helping Terry after he was having problems at the office. Terry admitted that he was feeling very insecure and upset. He had been believing that he was worthless and had been quite depressed. He had been working at a manufacturing company.

Terry was working one day when a co-worker said something about his hair. The co-worker meant it as a joke but Terry had been so fragile this set him off. Terry began to feel so sad that he left the office and had not been able to go back. He reached out for my help after missing several days of work.

I began to ask Terry if the hair comment was that bad. Terry told me that all the other person said was, "Wow, look at that hair." It didn't even seem that nasty or negative. Terry began to learn that his high level of insecurity was the reason he took this minor comment so seriously. We began to work on ways for Terry to improve his self-esteem.

Within a few months, Terry had been building his confidence. He practiced daily affirmations, had been taking care of his looks, doing physical workouts and finding time for fun. This led Terry to feel more optimistic about his work. He had even been finding that he was developing a few friendships with other staff. Terry admitted that he felt much happier knowing that he was able to feel connected with his company.

A big test came after about six months of our work together. Terry was feeling more joyous when one of his co-workers made fun of him. The old Terry would have become extremely hurt and upset. This time Terry laughed it off and did not take it to heart. He began to learn that sometimes a person says a mean comment because they are having a bad day, joking around or are insensitive. This would not derail the high amount of progress that Terry has been able to accomplish.

The workplace is filled with all different individuals. We must come together to achieve our work activities. You will be happier when you reach a place that you are not hurt when someone says something negative towards you. One great example is to look at a bully in school. The bully may be mean, say harmful words and put others down. It is important to understand that bullies are usually experiencing their own pain. There are not many who hurt others unless they are facing their own severe problems. Many bullies come from homes filled with rage, anger, sadness and despair. This does not justify their actions. It does help us to know that when someone is mean it usually is more about their own pain than yours.

It helps to learn that you do not have to let comments bring you down. We will also face times where someone says or does something that is hurtful. When we respond by not being upset, it helps us grow our abilities. You may discover that by letting go of a negative discussion you help to become less upset. It sometimes is an issue with your boss that has the power to shift your feelings.

I began to see Fred after he was put on work probation. Fred told me he blamed his supervisor Chris for all of his problems. Fred shared that Chris does not listen, orders him to do his work and is insensitive towards him. I then asked what issues Chris would say Fred should work on.

Fred shared that Chris always complains that Fred is often late. Chris is also upset that Fred has not been hitting his sales targets. The final complaint was Fred has become loud with Chris in front of the other workers. I ask Fred if Chris communicates the same way that he does. Fred starts to laugh and says, "Heck, no. Chris is the exact opposite of how I handle people." I began to explain that this is where the problem is occurring.

Fred wanted his boss to be the same as he is. He was wanting and needing his boss to be the same as he is. This may never happen. What we began to work on is how Fred can change to adapt to Chris. We start to learn that Fred had been inflexible and angry at his boss. This had caused all types of acting out, including being late. Fred began to realize that he must change his actions and his behaviors in the workplace.

I also taught Fred how to accept other types of individuals. Fred began to understand that Chris had learned many different ways of looking at the world. This is not positive or negative but it must be understood. Fred has begun to try and do his work in the way that Chris asks. He also began to come on time and work to reach his sales targets. Within a few months, Chris and Fred become closer. They started to accept each other and work towards being a stronger team. This allowed them both to achieve success and to accept each other.

Please answer these questions either as a group or alone:

What were the issues Betty was facing?

How did Betty improve her relationship with others?

What are the positive changes that Terry learned to make?

How did Fred improve his relationship with his boss?

CHAPTER THIRTEEN

Consistency is Key

The beginning of an assignment is exciting. The work is fresh and you may feel happy to work on something new. How many begin a job feeling enthusiastic, positive and ready for the new position? Why do some of us lose that feeling and begin to become negative and unhappy with our work? The lessons in consistency allow us to reach a higher potential and to improve our long-term success.

The best athletes, investors, leaders and teachers are both persistent and consistent. This means waking up each day and placing their full efforts in their chosen occupation. You will find many of these accomplished individuals keep working when they are tired, sad, confused, angry or have been failing. They have gained a great key to lasting achievement. It is to keep moving forward no matter what else is happening. We can always find an excuse to not place effort and accept defeat.

Where do we find the inner strength to keep going through developing our outlook. When we are working at a job there are always going to be obstacles. The person who keeps going will find that they are a valuable member of their team. We all depend on each other within the companies we work with. When you are dependable it improves the business as well as your own view of yourself.

I was helping a business that was trying to grow. They had hired many sales reps and were trying to expand into new markets. There was a worker, Juan, who was in his 40s. He began to apply for the job and was given an interview. He completed the meeting and was brought onto the team. Juan spent a week training and learning the role of a sales executive. Juan was supposed to begin working the following Monday. Juan made a call to his boss that he had a stomach ache. The boss asked if he would be able to work. Juan said he would not and he did not attend the first day of work.

Juan then needed to seek some medical care for his stomach issues. His boss told him to call him when he was feeling better. One month later, Juan called his boss and said he was feeling better. The boss was very warm and allowed Juan to start working again. They made a meeting for Monday at 10 a.m. The boss wrote to Juan at 9 a.m. Monday to confirm that Juan would be there. At 9:30 a.m., Juan wrote that he would not be attending. Should Juan be allowed to continue to be given a job? Did he appreciate that his boss gave him one month to deal with his health issues and he still was given another opportunity? Why didn't Juan call his boss to tell him that he could not make their meeting?

These interactions share how some workers handle their lives. They do not place the energy or effort in being there for their team. It is one thing to have a valid reason to be out of work. We cannot control if we face a health issue, loss of a loved one or have a major reason for missing our jobs. There are some workers who do not abide by this and try to take advantage of their companies. This usually leads to them either being let go or failing to accomplish their work.

There are ways to be consistent in our employment. It is to keep a positive outlook even during stressful times. You may also be willing to put in your full effort each day. When there is a rough patch in your work, you may still keep trying. This might mean asking in what ways you can contribute. You may ask your supervisor if there are any ways that you can help make things run smoother within the business. This leads to improved efficiency and greater respect for each worker.

I was helping a group and asked the manager to provide one example of the type of consistent worker that best illustrates pride within their position. The manager began to discuss John. John is a fifty-two year old account executive for this mid-size leather manufacturer. John had been with the business for over 17 years. He was dressed very professionally with a very nicely combed head of hair and glasses. The manager said that John was always trying to put in his full effort. I then asked what are some of the ways John is making positive choices.

The manager smiles and begins to list off a few of the ways John works. The boss said he arrived each day fifteen minutes before the start of work. Even though it sometimes snows in the winter, John leaves early on days that there might be traffic delays. The next step is that John was always the same with his workmanship. He consistently reached the upper target in terms of both number of sales calls along with deals closed. The next piece was that John was always helping his team. When someone had a question, John was always open to offering to help. John was always willing to adapt and change when his team shifts something. One example is when the computer system was upgraded and there were many workers angry and complaining. John did not become involved in this fight and learned how to use the new system properly.

The final piece of the manager's details about John are how he dealt with sales slumps. There were times, usually in the summer, when business was going slow. Many other workers stop trying or grow upset. Many leave the job or make the environment stressful. John continued to keep trying and had a friendly attitude. He didn't become angry or upset when situations were not going his way. This consistent positive outlook helped him be a quiet leader within the business. He was an unsung hero because he kept plugging along and helped show the other staff how to properly handle business.

I was impressed to learn about John and hear it described in front of the group. I then asked John why he behaved in this manner. Was there something unique or different about how he looked at life? John began to share that he had learned to ride the waves of work life. He believed that growing upset or angry only made his life harder. John also shared that his family taught him to take pride in everything they do. This meant placing his full efforts in a job. John always worked to the best of his ability because he took pride in what he did. John also believed that we earn our own reputation. He was not looking for accolades but allowed his actions to quietly speak for themselves.

This is a shining example of how dependability helps us to shine through. It is not always the person with the loudest voice that is heard the clearest. Your actions show if you are dependable and reliable. When you place the effort in learning to place your full effort you are likely to see success. You will also find that limiting negativity and complaining help you develop your own character.

There may not be as much excitement when you focus on coming to work on time each day, being kind to other staff and finding ways to be helpful. One of the strongest pieces of leadership is how you handle yourself. Your actions often speak much louder than your words. It helps to learn that becoming consistent, persistent and optimistic leads to a higher level of success.

Please answer these questions either as a group or on your own:

How does being persistent and consistent how us at work?

In what ways did Juan make poor choices in his new job?

What are three ways John shows he is a dedicated employee?

What are a few examples of how you could improve your own abilities through being consistent and keeping a positive attitude?

CHAPTER FOURTEEN

Overcoming Adversity

A winner is defined by how he deals with setbacks, sometimes, more than how often he wins. It is wonderful to feel the thrill of achieving your goal. What is better than closing a big deal, winning the big game or marking a major milestone? Our minds and bodies release chemicals that define these times of success. Who would not want more of one of the most positive feelings we are able to experience?

The true character of our soul is defined during the difficult times. The struggles often teach us and help us to find abilities we did not know we even held inside. I want to share a personal story to illustrate a few of these important points. It will help you to understand how the problems often turn around our lives.

There was a young man named Gerry. He was a hard worker and found a great amount of success. He was hoping to become a professional baseball player. Gerry is tall, athletic and strong. A great amount of his childhood had been focused on his goal. This included playing baseball for almost 6 hours each day. Gerry became a star on his little league team. He then became the top player on his travel team. It was not long before he was the number one baseball prospect at his high school.

Gerry was living a great life. The other students were all kind and wanted to be near Gerry. He was the star athlete and many believed he would become a professional major league player. The girls in his school all wanted to date Gerry because he was a celebrity in his hometown. The other boys were kind to him because they wanted to have his friendship. The teachers even showed him extra warmth because the school was seeing more interest in their sports program.

Gerry worked very hard to be the best baseball player. He also was having the time of his life. He loved playing his sport and it seemed as though Gerry had a charmed life. It didn't even feel very hard to continue to rise higher. This is when it all began to fall apart. The first problem was that Gerry's dad passed away. Gerry and his father had a huge connection and his dad was one of his biggest supporters.

The next problem happened during a spring training game. Gerry threw the ball during batting practice with another player. He felt a pop and his arm was severely injured. Gerry was told that it would take several major surgeries to repair his arm. This would mean a minimum of six months without being able to play. Was Gerry's charmed life falling apart? His father died suddenly and then an injury was stopping him from playing. Was it possible to get any worse? The answer was yes.

Gerry is then feeling upset and confused. He started to have mood swings and was struggling to be around others. One night, Gerry punched his wall and his mom feared he was going to hurt her. Gerry was put in a mental hospital and diagnosed with bipolar disorder. He now had to deal with facing a mental illness, therapy and a lifelong medication regimen. How would you feel if you were Gerry? His dreams had been shattered, his father was dead and he was now learning that he was mentally ill.

There was an important choice for Gerry to think over. He could have more than enough reason to accept defeat. He went from thinking he was going to be a major leaguer to feeling like a major loser. This led Gerry to think about his dad who had died. His father taught him a very important lesson, which he remembered. His dad said, "You will, at some point, feel as if your world has fallen apart. It may seem that everything has come against you. This is the time to stay so positive and work slowly to regain your life."

It hit Gerry like a ton of bricks. His dad's advice would lead him through the darkness. He began to attend therapy and work on his problems. Gerry also began to seek help for his arm injury. It was determined that Gerry would no longer be able to play baseball with the intensity that he was able to do before. He decided to develop a new dream and wanted to go to college to study teaching.

With a high level of effort, Gerry finished high school. He started college learning about becoming a high school teacher. Gerry focused on his new life and let go of the failures he had faced. He put the same level of effort into his studies and learning of how to teach others. It was clear Gerry had found his next area to focus on. He ended up becoming a teacher at one of the best schools in his hometown. There are many who find hope and learn from Gerry's wonderful work helping others.

Gerry admitted that is was hard to lose his dream. It taught him that anything can go away. When you are hit with huge problems, it is up to us to decide how to respond. We will always have something we can do to stay positive. This severe experience allowed Gerry to grow up, gain true strength and led to him finding his true calling. It was not easy, but Gerry appreciated the major lessons this taught him.

The work arena will often give us problems that test our ability. One example are layoffs within the business that lead workers to fear for their jobs. There are also times where sales are slow and you wonder if you can be successful in the work. The way to handle adversity is to learn to have measured responses. You may feel nervous, upset, confused or hopeless. The way you deal with these feelings will decide how you progress through the problems.

When there is stress how do you respond? Many will use drugs, alcohol, food addiction or other ways to soothe their feelings. The problem is that these are only temporary solutions that do not lead to long term improvement. There are many who have dealt with problems through addictive means and end up losing everything. The only way to move forward is to keep a positive attitude. This means finding some way to see the positive, even when the skies are dark all around you.

I began to see a man named Uri. He was a fantastic sales person and loved working. Uri was usually confident, optimistic and loved his work. During the past few months, there had been many changes within the company. This included 3,000 workers being let go and rumors that many others will soon be fired. Uri felt the fear among his staff and it was hard to not be nervous. Many of the other workers talked about being fired every day. The other problem is sales had been slowing. He was trying hard but he had not closed a deal in six weeks. This only added to his fears that he may be let go. Uri provided for his wife and three children. He barely made enough to support them and if he lost his job he didn't know how they would survive.

I talked with Uri and agreed that much of this situation was out of his control. He did not cause the layoffs that had been happening with his company. He also was trying his best to sell despite a hard climate. What could Uri do to improve these issues? The answer is that the unknown should not define him. If he spent each day fearful of losing his job this would not improve the issue. He didn't know what the management would do so why waste energy focusing on it?

Uri began to spend each day remembering what was working for him. He said, "I am happy I have a job today. I will do my best today to see success. I am putting in my full effort and will keep trying my hardest." This gave him a sense of peace and satisfaction. Uri liked his company and did feel happy to have a job. He also knew that putting in his best effort gave him a feeling of pride. Uri felt that working hard gave him something positive to focus on.

The way we deal with adversity will determine our outcome. When we grow angry and bitter it doesn't make the problem leave. It actually invites more issues and pain to enter in your life. Do you know that all of us have a justification for feeling bad? Every human being has experienced difficult and painful problems. There is a justified excuse for why someone is mean, negative, unhappy and addicted. This will only lead to a road filled with problems and pain.

There is a choice to make each day. It is to wake up and focus on what is working in your life. You may begin with feeling happy you are alive another day. You may also be appreciative that you have a job and are being paid to work. There are so many basic positive items in our lives. Do you have clean water to drink, food in your cabinet, and a place to live? There are some very simple ideas that will help you remember how to stay happy even when problems arise in your life.

Please answer these questions either as a group or alone:

Gerry began to face problems. What issues did he have to face?

Gerry began to rebuild his life. What positive steps did Gerry take to move forward?

Why is how you respond to problems important?

What issues did Uri face at his job? How did he handle them?

When you face adversity, why is your attitude important?

Please name three reasons you are thankful today?

CHAPTER FIFTEEN

Dedication Leads to Long Term Success

It is wonderful to read stories that say, "She became a movie star when she was found walking in the mall." "He started a business and before he knew it he was a billionaire." "The company started in a garage and now is the biggest tech company in the world." There may be a grain of truth in these but it usually removes the hard work that leads to accomplishment.

I have met and studied many of the most successful individuals. I was curious how many of them were able to achieve their goals. The clear answer was that dedication to their work is usually the key ingredient to finding success. What does it mean to be dedicated to your career? This usually includes being consistent and trying to not miss many days. It is also the characteristic of putting in your best effort. You do not have to be told to work or try hard in order to take action. It is the ability to be self-motivated that leads to long term success.

There are also many companies and individuals who rise and fall. Once in a while, a person does reach a high level through some type of lucky break. It may be a relative helps them obtain the job. There may be a person who starts a business and the idea happens to be in a "hot" industry. When you obtain quick success, it will only lead to long-term achievement through persistent efforts.

I have been interested in writing books since I was around 12 years old. When I was fourteen, I made national news trying to meet President Clinton. I was the hot story of the week and was invited to meet President Clinton in the Oval Office. I was 15 and decided I wanted to write a book. Due to the fact that I was appearing on many media outlets, it was easy for me to reach agents and publishers. Within a few days, I spoke with Simon and Schuster, Random House, St. Martins Press and many others. I found a literary agent and went on the meetings. They were all kind and interested in what I was presenting.

When the story was no longer in the news, my book had less value. The publishers chose to pass on publishing the book. I then persisted and published the book on my own with the help of an agent. I began a very long road to being an author. I spent many months promoting the first book at 15. I appeared on Entertainment Tonight, Maury Povich, The Daily News and many other media outlets.

I kept writing and working on books. I spent another 10 years trying to find a publisher for my books. I had several proposals written and sent to agents and publishers. During this time, I published another book on my own helping families improve their mental health. I kept writing and being dedicated to my work. I would eventually have my book Beating Bipolar published by a top publisher. I spent over two years writing and promoting this book. I travelled on my own dime to over 40 cities to do talks at chapters of The National Alliance on Mental Illness and The Depression and Bipolar Support Alliance. I also created thousands of pages online where readers would be able to find and buy my books. I also made 450 YouTube videos to promote the books and gain a wider audience.

When my book sells millions of copies, the press may choose to call me an instant millionaire. The fact are that it is over 20 years of efforts and persistence that finally allows me to find success in my chosen arena. It sounds sexier to say I wrote a book and it sold millions of copies around the world. This is usually not the case for anyone who finds lasting success.

Our work ethic has a great amount of determining how we handle our lives. It is easy to be lazy and waste our time. This is a dark pit that stifles your potential and abilities. When you are dedicated to your work, it means you continue to press through no matter what happens. I was speaking with a friend who runs a business with about 200 employees. He works 7 days a week and usually 12 hour days. I once asked him if he ever misses work.

He shared that he often has days he wakes up sick, tired, or feeling worn out. It is in these moments he tells himself he wants to be a leader. He gets dressed and heads to work no matter how he is feeling. He also chooses to be positive and helpful even on days he is sad or weak. This is his definition of what it means to be dedicated to his company. He also shared that his original plan was to build a big business and sell it within a few years. This would mean a great amount of money and allow him to pursue other areas. When the business took well longer to achieve success, he remained focused and determined. His choice is to be a warrior and stay strong no matter how long the battle lasts. Do you feel if he achieves his goals that his dedication was one of the reasons it worked out?

We all fall into traps of thinking something will make us happy. It may be a promotion, closing a deal, selling a business or anything else that we are hoping for. The truth is, even if we hit the goal, there will always be something else we want to achieve. The human mind is conceived to always want something new. You may have ten amazing watches but when you see a new one, your mind will likely hope to acquire it. This even is true for those not interested in material gain. If you love taking walks in nature your mind will be focused on when you can again go on the trail you enjoy. This is not negative or positive but it teaches that we must keep going.

The most dedicated team learns to work together. You may feel that others you work with are lacking something. It may be warmth, being helpful or that they judge you. When you look past someone's faults, you often find that they have something valuable to offer. The person who is always pushy teaches us the importance of standing up for ourselves. When you find someone who is a gossip, we learn the validity in holding our tongue. You may find someone who is always complaining and they teach you what it looks like to have a negative attitude. We are all able to grow and learn from those around us. Many of the uncomfortable feelings we experience are because certain individuals understand how to push our buttons. This teaches us how to learn to find ways to not become angry or upset.

I was helping a woman Joan who had been struggling to maintain her job selling clothes. She felt hurt that one of her supervisors said that she did not seem dedicated to her job. I asked her to explain and she began to admit that she had been late many times and had left work early on several occasions. We started to discuss why she was behaving this way. Joan began to share that she was struggling emotionally. She felt tired and didn't really want to work. She was only coming to this job because her family wanted her to work.

Joan began a long road to find her true path. She started work in a new company and changed her behavior. This included arriving 10 minutes early and always working to her highest potential. The new job allowed her to take one break and she used this time to meditate. Joan also had started to make new friends and felt comfortable in her job. Joan began to accept that seeking help is a way to be dedicated to positive choices. When she worked out her own issues, she was ready to see more success.

We often experience a wake-up call that shows us we have to change. This may be a supervisor catching you behaving poorly, a co-worker saying something about your actions or being disciplined. When these problems arise, it is your decision how you respond. The most important question is are you willing to be dedicated to your work. If you do not want the job, there are many others who would love your position. You waste your own time when you do not place your full efforts and energies in your job.

When you are hardworking, determined, persistent, passionate and positive you become a leader. Your behaviors impact everyone who encounters you. They begin to try harder because they see how much effort you are placing in your work. There are also many new opportunities and promotions when staff see someone placing their energies into their work. Every business wants to cultivate the staff and team members that are willing to do their best work. You may learn to develop your gifts by staying focused and helping your team.

Please answer these questions either as a group or alone:

The author has been persistent in writing books. What are a few reasons he has found success?

When the business owner is tired in the morning does he go to work? Why does he do this?

What does Joan do differently in her new position?

What are the reasons it is important to be dedicated to your job?

Please name three ways hard work leads to success in our careers?

CHAPTER SIXTEEN

Make Today Count

This moment is the one we are experiencing. There is a great strength in learning to find peace and joy at this particular period of time. The past is over and tomorrow continues to be an unknown. You have a decision to make this day the best one possible. How do we let go of our fears and the blocks that hold us back from staying centered and present?

It appears that many species are only focused on the now. When you view a tiger, bear, deer or other animal they are most likely not worried about their past. They also do not sit around and worry if the stock market will rise, how they can afford another vacation or why their family hurt their feelings. In a way, they are blessed to not have a mind that is highly analytical and developed to analyze different situations. In humans, it is both a positive and a negative that we have a highly developed brain.

I began to work with a man named Emmitt. He was hoping to learn to stay calm and release his fears. Emmitt was always thinking about how his marriage had ended and he was single. He spent a great amount of time worrying about his future. This included fears that he will lose his job, that he will always be alone and that his health will begin to fail. This constant state of anxiety made his days very long. He also struggled to concentrate on his work and keep up with his responsibilities.

It was clear that Emmitt was having a rough time. We began to develop a few ways to change his thought patterns. The first assignment was for him to go into something with a great amount of natural beauty. He found a local hiking trail that had beautiful green trees, purple flowers, birds, ducks and many species. Emmitt took a long walk around this trail and his goal was to look at everything around him. He began to feel calm and peaceful. Emmitt also reported that during this time he was not thinking about anything that was around him.

I asked Emmitt what it felt like when he was in the moment. He sharee that it was the first time in a while that he was not nervous. He didn't focus on the problems and issues in his life.

Emmitt said he actually felt free and weightless. Our goal was to help him learn to feel this way upon his own command. I then began to teach Emmitt about meditation. I shared with him about envisioning being in the nature trail with his eyes closed. The goal was to have a mental picture of the park and to feel as though he was actually there.

Emmitt began to practice and within a few weeks was confident in seeing the trail in his head. We begin to speak that he can take a few moments each day to close his eyes and see himself there. This helped Emmitt while he was working. He said when he felt nervous he took a moment to envision the trail. This allowed him to change the channel in terms of the anxiety and restlessness. The value in this skill was that he can decide to stop the toxic thoughts from taking over his mind.

Did you ever think why today is a gift? How many ways are you able to see the joyous parts of your own life? Here are a few simple ideas of why we are lucky to have this day. Many of you have a job, food, place to live, friends, family, a way to be productive, hobbies and are healthy enough to work. These are all very valuable and not everyone has the ability to have this much positivity in their lives. The reason to be thankful is that you are able to learn that this is an important day.

I began to help Farrah when she was feeling depressed. She has been working in a marketing company for the last 2 years. She said she was starting to lose her passion for life and didn't really know what to do. I then asked her about her favorite activities to spend her time. Farrah admitted that she no longer spent time on herself. Farrah worked, came home and took care of her elderly mom, cleaned the house and then went to sleep. She had lost the piece of herself that craved joy and happiness.

Farrah and I talk about what she used to enjoy doing. She admitted that in college she was passionate about painting. She would draw beautiful charcoal drawing and use watercolors. This period of her life was one of her happiest times. Farrah would also go on weekends to a karaoke bar and sing pop music. She no longer did any of this.

I began to share how important it was for Farrah to take care of herself. If she did not find activities she enjoyed, her life would become depressing. We started a plan for her to take an art class one night each week. She also joined a group where they go every Saturday to do karaoke. The first night was a blast. Farrah sang Madonna songs and connected with her new friends. Within a few months, she was no longer depressed. She had found her joy and was learning to again love her life.

Farrah was now able to concentrate at her job. She had a new passion and joy about her life. Farrah was learning that taking care of yourself is one of our most important roles. She was also making the best of each day. She no longer felt guilty for having fun. This was one of the most important pieces of living. You must find the activities you are passionate about and spend time pursuing them. We all have gifts and talents that should be explored. Are there any new activities you might want to try that would allow you to find more excitement? Is there something you used to do that was fun that might again be worth doing?

I was walking around a retail store yesterday to buy my son a toy car. I noticed a few of the sales staff were working and they looked pretty down. One worker was walking down the aisle with a smile on his face. He smiled at me and said, "How are you doing?" His whole attitude and friendliness made me feel better. I also watched as he interacted with his co-workers by being helpful and kind. This is an example of a worker making the best of this day. He has learned that being warm to others improves the environment.

There are some easy ways to be kinder around the office. You may choose to ask others how they are doing. When you smile and are willing to listen you make each day better. The teams that are filled with caring staff make more progress. Your attitude has a ripple effect on those you interact with. It is within your potential to make each day one where we give it everything we have.

One other major part of enjoying the day is to not let a bad moment ruin your whole experience. I came into my office to write and work today. I am in a fairly happy mood and everything has been going well. I then lost about a page of writing which was accidentally deleted. I made a conscious effort to not grow upset. I started again and rewrote the page. A few minutes later, I answered my phone. When I walked to my desk, I banged my knee very abruptly on the table. It hurt and I was frustrated. I again decided to not let this ruin my day. I have began to remember and focus on why I am happy to be here. It is a great skill to let the minor problems we experience not make us upset and angry. The best days are the ones where we remember all the reasons this is a wonderful day and opportunity for growth.

Please answer these questions either as a group or alone:

What fears did Emmitt have?

How did Emmitt change his thinking?

Farrah began to enjoy life again. What were the ways she learned to find more happiness?

What did the worker at the retail store do to help improve his environment?

What are a few ways you are able to make the best of this day?

How does overcoming problems help you improve your job?

CHAPTER SEVENTEEN

Enjoying Work is a Choice

When you walk into your job how do you start your day? What does it feel like when someone walks into their office with a grumpy disposition, complaining about being there and having a negative attitude about work? I was reading a book that shared a wonderful educational lesson on this very topic. The book detailed a party with many in attendance. During the event, many are tired, unhappy, and complaining amongst themselves.

A man walks in with a big smile on his face. He began to use his charisma to speak to others with a fun and excited demeanor. This person is known as the life of the party and their way of being changes the whole event. There now seems to be a more positive mood and many begin to have a great time. Did this one person somehow change the entire feeling within a large gathering? The answer is even one motivated, kind, charismatic and helpful person has the ability to shift many others.

You may decide to walk into work with a great attitude. It will help if you start talking about all the reasons you are feeling happy. You may discuss how coming to work is one of the best parts of your life. When you arrive on time, with a happy attitude, and are prepared to work you are shifting the workplace. You may even see that you're able to improve a large office by coming in with a pleasant manner.

I started helping Sandra after she returned to work after having her first child. She was finding it very hard to return to her company and have the same outlook she used to have. As a mother, she was now thinking about her new son for a good part of the day. I then, curiously, asked Sandra her motivation for returning to her job. Sandra said, "I came back to work because I need the money and benefits provided by this position." I then followed asking her if this was the only reason she had returned.

Sandra became upset and started to say that she used to love her job. She was enjoying working on interesting projects and being around smart team members. Sandra also enjoyed the many different types of people who work within her company. She was upset during her time off because she was usually alone with her child. We began to help her see that there are many wonderful parts of working. Sandra identified that her job had the ability to be a very positive part of her life.

I then start to learn about the real problems Sandra is facing. She was nervous that she cannot handle the pressure of being a mom and also holding her job. Sandra was struggling to balance all of the responsibilities she was experiencing. I then helped her to see that she would be able to adjust. Within a few weeks, she was comfortable in her dual roles as a mother and a worker. Sandra also chose to find positive parts of working. She began each day being thankful that she had a job. Sandra also focused on the parts of work she enjoyed. This helped her to see why working was often fun.

It is clear that sometimes we have to adapt and our lives face different hurdles. Each of us is different but, in many ways, we all face struggles. I remember when my brother died suddenly while I was working as a therapist at a treatment center. I used to always come into the office smiling, helping others, and being a team player. There were many who chose to complain but I would always try to be a light within the company. I would listen, support and find something positive to focus us.

When my brother died, my world was different. I had spoken to him on a Saturday and he was himself. We shared about many fun experiences in our lives and he was hoping to move closer to our family. He was working at a ski mountain helping with their maintenance crew. In the middle of the night, I was woken by my wife and 6 year old daughter. They told me he died. I thought I was having a bad dream. Could my only brother have actually died? I rose out of bed and was shaken. I quickly spent the next few days helping my family. We went to his funeral and came together to handle our loss. It was very hard to see my father tell me that he shouldn't have to bury a son. We were all struggling and handling our heavy emotions.

I was to return to work after two weeks from my brothers passing. I made a choice to be as helpful, supportive, kind and hard working as possible. I found that my team members were extremely warm and friendly towards me. They showed such love that I felt very grateful to be a part of their team. Many of the patients I worked with also were very kind. I was able to see that returning to my work was a great way to move forward. I chose to focus on all of the reasons that my job was a positive experience.

I'm being open about my loss because many times during work we will face some heavy situations. It may mean losing someone you love, facing a health condition, experiencing a financial problem, having a relationship issue or an experience that makes your life hard. I have seen how those who continue to have a positive work rise higher despite the obstacle. You may need to seek support for the problem you are facing. The reality is many times our work is a wonderful way to be productive. It also allows us to be connected to others. We may find that those in our work help us grow stronger and handle different situations.

I was helping a man named Justin who worked with a sales company. Justin told me that he always made a decision to arrive at his job and improve the environment. This included listening to others, sharing positive feedback, staying motivated and being willing to learn. Justin was one of the most successful sales executives. I observed him to be extremely friendly, warm, and you can feel his positive energy. I wondered if Justin's life was completely easy and always went well.

Justin began to share in therapy that he was always optimistic. Even with his great outlook, he had faced many tough situations. This included a time when he was struggling financially after going through a divorce. He ended up losing his home to foreclosure and had to file for bankruptcy. Justin also lost both his mom and dad in the same year, which was very trying. This was on top of Justin going through a severe bout of depression that led him to face a one-month hospital stay. I was curious at how Justin put all of these problems behind him to become a leader in business.

He spoke of how, during the hard teams, it may seem very rough. Justin knew he had a laundry-list of reasons why he could give up. When his dad died, he remembered the lesson his father always spoke about. It is that no matter what happens, we can pick ourselves up and start again. His gift was to teach his son that he could keep trying and press through his problems and pain.

It only took a few years before Justin was able to rebuild his life. He kept a great attitude and found he is a gifted salesperson. He would begin to make a great living and be able to rebuild from the financial hole he fell into. Justin even met a new woman and they were able to enjoy a wonderful marriage. Justin had learned that he will always find the reasons to focus on what is working within his job. He felt lucky to be able to have a way to support himself and remembers the struggles he overcame. This was one of the reasons Justin had learned to be a success. He didn't let his darkest times turn him into a negative failure. This led him to make different choices and find the winner that was within his mind, body and soul.

Please answer these questions either as a group or on your own:

How did the man who walks in the party with a very positive attitude change the environment?

What are some of the reasons Sandra learns to be appreciative of her job?

What are the ways staying positive helps us face a difficult situation?

How did Justin rebuild his life?

What are some ways you could demonstrate coming to work with a positive attitude?

CHAPTER EIGHTEEN

Learning to Reach Your Full Potential

Did you know that it is possible for you to reach a higher level within your life? When you care about your work you are proving that you are ready for success. It is possible that a high level of effort makes a difference in the outcome of your own life. You may feel that what you are doing is not valuable but this is false.

There are two workers who both start working at an ice cream parlor. They are both in college and have taken the job as a way to help pay for school. One of them is named Taylor and she sees this position as an opportunity for growth. She comes to the shop early, is very kind to all the customers, cleans the ice cream with a great outlook and is an all-around all-star. Taylor began to learn about sales, running a retail location and dealing with customers.

The other young woman at the ice cream parlor is Nancy. She is unhappy that she has to work. Nancy thinks it is a waste of her time and she is only there for the cash. Nancy had a tough summer because of her bad attitude. She ended up being fired, which caused her to have a cash-flow problem. Nancy ended up not being able to pay for college because she didn't have enough money to survive. Her behavior didn't seem important but it led to many problems in her life.

Taylor's work led to something wonderful. She completed the summer and chose to obtain a degree in business management. Taylor was able to apply her skills to run a retail location. Within a few years, Taylor was a regional manager for a large restaurant operation. She made a huge salary and was rising quickly within the business.

These two young women both started with the same simple job. One chose to reach their highest potential where they were. The other saw the job as a waste of time. They ended up ruining their life because they didn't reach their potential. There are no small jobs. When you work it is up to you to reach your full level of skill. It may appear that an entry-level job does not serve a purpose in your life. The facts are many of the greatest financial and business leaders started in a mailroom, serving fries, cleaning toilets, and many other positions. Please know where you are right now is not the final outcome.

What does it mean to reach your full potential in a position? I find the level of your success comes down to your attitude, efforts and how you treat others. Do you place your highest level of work even when nobody is watching? Do you try hard even when you don't get anything extra for your efforts? A winner in life is usually someone that learns to care about all aspects of their lives. They develop their abilities by being the best in everything they do. You may find that what you are doing today has a large impact on where you end up in your life. Will you show persistence, dedication, cleanliness, and a positive attitude? These are the backbone of being a success.

I have had the honor of helping many types of individuals at different aspects of their lives. I know that each person has an ability to rise higher and set their own personal goals. I often learn from the lessons my clients have taught me over the years.

Jack was a talented computer programmer. He had risen from an entry-level job at his software company to being one of the senior programmers. I was curious how Jack rose to his high level of employment. Jack shared he was always curious. He started to learn programming by taking classes in the evening. It wasn't long before most of his free time was spent learning the language of computers. Even when he had a high level of skill, he kept trying to learn new technologies. His efforts continue to payoff. He is considered a huge asset to his company. Jack knows how to help many different technical and often complex computer issues that his business needs to understand. There is something even more important than his robust computer skills.

Many of the staff do not understand computers the way that Jack does. Jack is so kind, helpful and is a wonderful teacher. He calmly explains many of the lessons to help others on his team. He even started a computer training class to help educate and teach others in his company about new skills. The feeling around the office about Jack is extremely high. He never causes tension, is always willing to help and keeps a great attitude. This also includes that he almost never misses work and is always on time and willing to work late. He is so dependable that even the CEO began to learn about his work.

This is the reason Jack has climbed so high and quickly. He developed his own abilities and worked to help others rise higher. He was a quiet leader who showed his ways with positive actions. It is easy to understand why Jack earns a high salary and has been given a number of promotions. You do not have to be a computer programmer to rise through the ranks within your business. I began to work with a woman name Allie who only was able to finish high school. Allie struggled with school but was willing to work. She began to find a job cleaning offices. Allie started to work at a large company that had a gigantic series of buildings and offices. Allie always worked extra hard and was putting in her highest level of efforts. A few examples include that she folded the toilet paper in the bathroom and made it look very presentable and neat. She also dusted areas of the ceiling and parts of the office that many cleaners did not approach. Allie also scrubbed out any stains she noticed and was always being helpful to the other cleaners.

In a few months, many of the cleaning team started to talk about Allie. They all noticed how dedicated and motivated she was. When an assistant manager of cleaning role opened, Allie was nominated. She accepted the new job, higher pay and more responsibility. In this job, Allie put even more effort into her work. Within a few years, Allie was made the head of a staff of 400 cleaning people. This came with a huge annual salary, retirement benefits, paid vacation, full medical insurance and many features. The hard work had paid off for Allie. She had allowed her efforts to help her reach her highest potential.

There are no jobs that are not important. If you are a secretary, be the greatest one they have ever seen. If you are a janitor, clean with the passion and efforts that will help you stand out. When you work in sales, be the best salesperson the company has ever seen. You may be serving fries but do it with passion, enthusiasm and joy. We all are able to rise higher in whatever we are doing. What would your company accomplish if every one of the team practiced placing their full efforts in everything? You would find that the business will thrive and each team member will rise to a higher level!

This is the day to improve how you place efforts in accomplishing more. There are ways you are able to improve. Even the greatest workers could find something to do better. Is there a new sale you could learn that would help you grow your knowledge? Is there a way you could work harder, smarter, with more effort and skill? What are the ways that you could develop your abilities and help your company achieve more?

You may have to look deep within to find the passion to try harder. If you are negative, you might not care about your job. Please know that the work you do each day has the power to define your future. When you are placing the highest level of effort and skill in your work it helps you! A few reasons we fail in life is due to laziness, wasting others times, squandering opportunities and not being fully present in each activity we are placed in. You can change these toxic ways by finding the courage to place more effort in all of your work.

Please answer these questions either as a group or on your own:

Taylor and Nancy both are working in an ice cream parlor. How are their attitudes different? Why did Taylor's experience help her life?

In what ways is Jack a leader within his company?

Allie found a high level of success. What did she do to achieve her goals?

What are a few reasons people fail in their lives?

What steps can you take today to improve your abilities?

CHAPTER NINETEEN

We Are All a Team

When you work within a company, you have a mission. Each member is part of a team that is striving for success. The clearest goal of companies are to become more profitable and obtain a larger market share. There are many important ways that businesses create products or services that are needed in our world. What would we do if we could not buy food, drive in cars, have a home or the many other industries that produce the items we desire?

The largest part of achieving a balanced staff is that every person realizes they are important. There are no small jobs and without each person doing their part many businesses would not survive. I have been a witness how certain companies have created a culture that allows everyone to feel valuable, unique and that their gifts are important. It is within these businesses that we feel hopeful, joyous and dedicated to our careers. We all have an inner need to feel that our lives are serving an important purpose. This intangible feeling is one of the greatest indicators of how much we enjoy our work.

I began to help a watch company improve their team skills. They were having some problems after the market they were in began to shrink. There was a round of layoffs and many had lost the original excitement towards working. We began to look at where the company started. It all began with one man who had a remarkable passion for creating beautiful watches. His life was dedicated to crafting the most stylish and sleek watches of his time. This grew from his home into large offices in many cities around the world.

I started to ask the workers what they would hope to see change within the business. Many share that they used to have managers that would create goals, structure and teamwork. They would know what their sales targets were and many would come together trying to achieve these numbers. In the last few months, the staff felt that they had been in survival mode. They were all worried about being fired and the company had not had the same enthusiasm they used to feel.

I then asked, "How can you do your best work when you don't know if your job will be there in 3 months?" Many admitted this is the feeling they are having in their minds and hearts. They do not know how stable the business is and are fearing for their own future. We admitted that this is a hard issue and there is not a simple answer. We then began to look at what would happen if each member of the team did their best each day. This would mean placing a higher level of effort, connecting with other workers, having a positive attitude and helping each other.

They all agree that this would be a better way to work. If they chose to fall into a state of fear then nothing would be accomplished. They could also lose their market edge if all the team is not focused on growing the business. It took time but they began to take things day-by-day. Many developed a new outlook and stayed optimistic. It was a long road forward that eventually led them to achieve higher sales. During this time, one of the design team made a new watch that became a new leader in market share. The designer had the courage to keep creating even in a state of uncertainty. What happens if we as a company or society stop progressing? If we do not move forward then the obvious path is only backward. Why would we want to fall behind when we are able to rebuild.

I have been able to learn a great amount about the psychology of business and how our minds handle different lessons. One of our greatest issues is learning to overcome fear. We can be nervous about our health, financial success, future and relationships. The part of fear that is the most difficult is there is always a way to justify these emotions. You can look at the world or watch the news and there will definitely be problems that would allow us to be fearful. You may also have experiences or life situations which are making life hard.

I used to have many fears that held me back. I would use the excuse that this is the reason for my laziness or that I am justified in not placing my highest level of efforts. This only made my situations and problems harder. It took until I would no longer let my feelings stop me from moving towards my goals. I became a highly successful speaker, author and coach by working hard each day. I wake up with a wonderful outlook because this is the secret to my success. I have obtained so many accomplishments because I will always have a way to brighten those I work with. When you combine being poised, focused, driven, optimistic, enthusiastic and happy, you have the recipe for winning in our work. It is also the factor of how marriages last, friendships grow and we eventually are able to mentor others. You are able to be the part of your team that helps us improve our lives.

I know that many teams are often learning to adapt. I had a great discussion yesterday with a successful real estate agent. He shared how, for many years, his role has been to work with large corporations and to help them find retail properties for their business. He has helped many teams and learned a great amount during his 40 years of work experience. One of the best lessons he discussed is that we sometimes must develop patience. There have been many times where big businesses would take many months to formulate a decision. They have several teams that would analyze and try to decide the best way forward.

You may be a part of a big company where there are lots of rules and structure. It may seem that it takes a long time for any change to happen. When you become patient and continue to place your best efforts it is developing your character. It is also teaching that sometimes there will be a long gap between what you hope to improve and it being implemented within the business. You may sometimes feel frustrated but patience helps you handle almost any situation.

I have found that many great team members are those that learn to be unshakable. They do not get angry when a situation does not go their way. They also don't get frustrated when new ways of working or different rules are implemented. The adaptable team member is one of the most important assets to a business. There will always be new pieces of business that cause different adjustments. The way you respond to these issues will help define your character and cement your reputation within your team.

It is not always easy to be willing to go with the flow and not create tension. What does it feel like when a worker grows hostile, is negative or gives up trying to work hard? It begins to deflate those around them and worsens the situation. The opposite is a team member who always finds a reason to be positive, places their full effort in the job and is willing to change with the new procedures. You are able to become the positive worker. This allows you to find more success and reach a higher place of learning.

Please answer these questions either as a group or on your own:

Why are all workers important?

How does overcoming fear help us in our work?

Why is patience important in our work?

What are a few ways to be a positive team member?

What are three ways you are able to improve how you work with your team?

CHAPTER TWENTY

The Road to a Brighter Future

The road of life is a very long journey. Your work career will also have many different lessons and experiences. The way you handle your behavior will be a major factor on how your life turns out. I have had the honor of helping many experiencing all types of life situations. This includes individuals facing brain cancer, depression, bipolar disorder, urological cancer, heart attacks, losing parents, children, friends and going through divorce.

I found within each person's life there is a common thread that determines our future. When you learn to see life through optimistic eyes it gives you the courage to continue. There are times in each of our lives where we feel the floor has fallen out. It is during those toughest moments and experiences that our true strength is built. When my brother died last year at age 27, I developed a new found strength. I have worked for many years teaching others to be positive but could I practice what I preached? Would I be able to keep a positive attitude when some of the most dramatic problems all appeared at once? I decided to keep smiling, trying and pressing forward. During this time, I wrote a book helping others with mental illness and addiction. I worked helping those in work and other settings who were struggling emotionally. I educated at numerous organizations. The best lesson was that I do not have to have a perfect life to help impact others.

You may also have faced a series of setbacks. It is likely that you have felt down and worried about your career and life. The best way to improve how we work is to see a light at the end of the tunnel. Your future depends on how you handle this moment. It is a choice to find a way to improve each day. Even when you grow negative, it is possible to stop from letting these emotions take over.

You have a power and energy within your mind and body. The best way to improve life is to stay mentally and physically healthy. This means making healthy food decisions, doing frequent physical activities, keeping positive and being able to bounce back. I was listening to a tape sharing about how storms often come into the world. Many times during a weather event, lots of trees will fall down and die. The palm tree has a remarkable ability to bend during a storm. It will look as though the palm is about to break. It rarely does and will eventually stand up straight once the rough weather has passed.

It is within your potential to be similar to the palm tree. Even during the storms of our lives, we can bend and not break. This means not falling into addiction or other ways of ruining our body.

You can then progress past the difficulty and be ready for when the improved environment has arrived. There are many who understand that business has various cycles. You must learn to stay strong no matter what is happening in the moment. It is likely that the problems of today will be different or gone by tomorrow. Your attitude and outlook are the key ingredients for turning around your life.

I chose to call this book The Positive Worker because you are now ready to fill those shoes. It is within your power to come to work each day with a great attitude. You may find the strength to learn, develop your abilities and be the best possible worker. I find that those who try the hardest often are the ones who achieve the greatest success. You may one day be able to mentor another person to teach them the skills you have developed.

My favorite part of my life is allowing my knowledge to educate others. I have been able to help many who are willing and open to change. You are able to rise higher, achieve more and become the positive worker.

I know when you keep growing and stay hopeful anything is possible. You may, one day, rise to lead a company or help impact others' lives. It is often that the greatest leaders have learned the lessons that they teach. You are well prepared to find success on the road to the future. I appreciate you allowing me to help you learn to enjoy the journey. We are all part of a team and when we work together we are able to achieve the highest level of accomplishment. You are now ready for the road that lies ahead.

Please answer these questions either as a group or on your own:

What are some of the lessons you have learned from this book? What are a few ways you can improve how you handle your job? Please share some of your thoughts and feelings after completing this book?

<u>We Want to Hear from You!</u>

If your company or group is interested in having Blake LeVine speak at your business or organization we welcome you to call our offices at (213) 304-9555. We also offer bulk orders for events and groups. Blake offers a coaching program to assist both workers and executives. Please feel free to reach out at any time at the above number. The author also welcomes any feedback, suggestions or emails and you may submit these to him at blakelevinecoach@gmail.com. Thank you for purchasing this book and we hope you have enjoyed it.

www.ingramcontent.com/pod-product-compliance
Lightning Source LLC
Chambersburg PA
CBHW080807180526
45168CB00006B/2356